Resolving Community Conflict:
an annotated bibliography

by Anne Osborne Kilpatrick

Institute of Community and Area Development
The University of Georgia

Resolving Community Conflict:
an annotated bibliography

Annotations: Anne Osborne Kilpatrick
Editing: Nancy Condon, Rebecca McCarthy
Research: Nancy Condon, Lisa Honigberg, Rodger Brown
Cover: Reid McCallister

Copyright 1983 by the Institute of Community and Area Development, The University of Georgia. All rights reserved. No part of this publication may be used or reproduced in any manner whatsoever without written permission. For information, contact the Publications Program, ICAD, 300 300 Old College, The University of Georgia, Athens, Georgia 30602.

Library of Congress Cataloging in Publication Data Pending
ISBN 0-911847-01-4

Foreword

    Conflict often results when community officials cannot meet demands for a redistribution of resources such as money, legal assistance or expertise. Handling conflict--resolving, managing, and regulating it--is becoming a necessary skill for community leaders.

    The Institute of Community and Area Development (ICAD) specializes in helping communities deal effectively with problems on a variety of levels. We help them assess several possible solutions--they decide what they should do.

    To promote this effort further, we began designing a publication that would help individuals from both the public and private sector work effectively in resolving differences. We wanted to produce a reference work that would highlight successful practices focused on managing problems peculiar to a community setting.

    <u>Resolving Community Conflict: an annotated bibliography</u> is the result of our labors. We hope it will prove to be a valuable aid for those dealing with community problems.

    The project is largely the work of Anne Osborne Kilpatrick, a doctoral candidate in public administration at the University of Georgia, specializing in organization development. Before beginning her advanced graduate studies, Kilpatrick worked as a professional planner and program administrator in health and human services for eight years. She also has had experience in management, labor relations, and community relations.

Albert F. Ike
ICAD Associate Director
September 1983

Acknowledgements

Many people have been instrumental in the creation of this work.

Dr. Albert F. Ike, the project director, has been enthusiastic, supportive, and committed to the project since its inception. The first to contribute to the bibliography, Dr. Margaret Herrman gave generously of her time and efforts in the developmental stages.

Several students have worked on the citations, spending many long hours searching the libraries in Athens and Atlanta to ensure accuracy of the sources. They are Lisa Honigberg, Rebecca Murrell, and Rodger Brown.

ICAD editorial assistant Nancy Condon is cited for her attention to painstaking detail and unlimited commitment to accuracy. Janet Walker decoded and transcribed hieroglyphics, taught me the technology of word processing, and shared her space.

Dr. Robert T. Golembiewski, my major professor and mentor, has given me copious support, valuable feedback, and comments on the project during the last two years. My editor, Rebecca McCarthy, encouraged and prodded me until I completed the work.

Appreciation goes to my parents, who taught me the importance of peacemaking, to my friends who reinforce our universal need for community, and to my sons, who I hope will inherit a peaceful world.

Anne Osborne Kilpatrick
September 1983

Table of Contents

Foreword.. iii

Acknowledgements.. iv

Matrices.. 5A, 5B, 5C

Annotations... 6

Citations... 40

PURPOSE

This document has been developed to serve as a resource to practitioners and academicians engaged in community conflict management and conflict resolution. The document has two parts:

1) The first section is a select annotated bibliography, organized alphabetically and catalogued in matrices. These are explained further in the text. Among the publications included in the annotated bibliography are reports of applications of new or different methods to resolve disputes and possible areas for future use and research. To illustrate the richness of the conflict resolution field, the annotations reflect works from a wide variety of disciplines. Most of the publications are dated from 1974, but important earlier works are also included.

2) The second part of the text is a larger, multidisciplinary bibliography on conflict. This section emphasizes those works published since 1974, but includes key works from earlier years as well. The entries have been organized in alphabetical order; each one includes all the information necessary for easily retrieving the publication.

INTRODUCTION

The issue of conflict resolution has concerned invididuals since time began, but community conflicts today seem more intense than in the past. Perhaps this intensity is due to the extremes that seem to be more prevalent today--between the 'haves' and the 'have-nots,' urban and suburban residents, the young and the old, men and women, parents and children--and to the richness of our ethnic, cultural, and religious backgrounds.

The rising crime rate instills in us a fear for our personal safety--and a dissatisfaction with our criminal justice system. This system often appears to focus more on the rights of the offender than on those of the victim, and frequently serves to convert a minor offender into a hardened repeater. The overloaded and backlogged court system is matched by overcrowded correctional institutions. Such facilities may protect the public from the criminals but apparently do little to rehabilitate them.

And what of the conditions of the communities from which these problems came? How are disputes resolved? Increasing numbers of alternative, nonjudicial methods are being introduced to handle the inevitable conflicts resulting from interaction in our hectic world. Many of these methods are included and described in this reference.

Other kinds of conflict frequently arise that must be addressed by community officials; for example, bargaining over budgets, establishing personnel procedures and benefits, resolving employee disputes, and addressing citizen problems over land use and public services. Such situations require special skills in several areas--interpersonal and group dynamics as well as organizational and systemwide applications. Hence, this bibliography on resolving community conflict includes information on these and other areas that may be useful to the reader.

DEFINITIONS:

The following general definitions were used in the select annotated bibliography. They structured the materials selected for this document.

Conflict is one of several states in which persons in a community can interact. According to Laue and Cormick (see Bermant, no. 7), actors and institutions in a community interact along a continuum that moves from cooperation to competition, conflict, and crisis.

Conflict is not considered to be a negative situation because it is present in virtually all situations. However, if conflict is allowed to proceed without management or resolution, the potential for violence is great. According to Laue and Cormick's model, the threat of crisis motivates the involved parties to resolve their conflict.

Sociologists agree that conflict often exists when an unequal distribution of resources exists (e.g., funds, time, manpower, access to the mass media, access to legal assistance, etc.) and when one involved party wants to redistribute the resources. In this case, another party wanting to maintain the status quo probably already has most of the power or resources.

Conflicts can be resolved in several ways. In a repressive environment, the more powerful member can simply dominate the less powerful member through the use of legal or forceful methods. This domination may serve only as a temporary solution. The crisis will more than likely reemerge at some future date when the frustrations of the less powerful member increase and the price of protest appears worth the possible gains.

Other methods exist to resolve conflict. Litigation is frequently used, often to the detriment of both parties because it can be both time-consuming and costly. In the litigation process, an impartial third party--a judge or an administrative tribunal--renders a decision. The feelings and emotions of the affected parties may nevertheless remain unchanged.

The decision creates a winner and a loser, thus keeping the two parties polarized. Since neither party was directly responsible for making the decision and, therefore, neither "owns" it, there is no assurance that both parties will abide by the decision. Enforcement of these kind of decisions has been a major problem in domestic relations. For example, judges often decide a divorcing husband's financial responsibility to his estranged wife and children; enforcing such decisions has been extremely difficult in our country.

Intervention involves a third party who assists the two disputants in resolving their conflict. According to Laue and Cormick (see Bermant, no. 7), this third may assume one of five roles: advocate, mediator, researcher, enforcer, or activist. It is important that the intervenor be clear on which role he or she is playing. The responsibilities and skills involved in each role, as well as the relationships with the conflicting parties, are quite different.

One way in which an intervenor may help the two parties in conflict resolve their differences is to establish a superordinate goal on which both parties can agree. Once this goal is identified and agreed upon, resolution of the immediate conflict is made easier.

Bargaining and negotiation are based on exchanges and agreements. Both have been utilized in the labor-management field to develop labor agreements or contracts and to avoid strikes, work stoppages, and violence. As unionization of the public sector increases, the method's importance will also increase. Alternatives to striking are crucial because public safety employees, as well as teachers, have joined the organized labor movement. Trust, openness, exchange, and commitment, are essential elements for effective negotiating.

Mediation is a form of voluntary intervention in which the conflicting parties select a third party to mediate their dispute. Aided by the mediator, the parties work out certain agreements. They are not always legally bound by these agreements, but they are morally committed to resolving their differences. Mediation is being used with increasing frequency in new environments as an alternative to litigation.

More structured than mediation, arbitration is generally binding on both parties. Unlike mediation, in which the decision is made jointly by the conflicting parties, arbitration shifts the responsibility of the final decision to the third party arbitrator. Currently, arbitration is most frequently used in labor-management conflicts. It is being adopted increasingly by family courts and local domestic courts in the form of both voluntary and compulsory arbitration.

Meeting-facilitation is a relatively new concept that could almost be called "conflict avoidance." Described by Doyle and Strauss (see no. 30), this method strives to obtain the best decisions possible by having the participants involved in potentially controversial activities reach a consensus, or a lack of disagreement on the issues. In this process, the facilitator controls the group's interactions and assists members in making quality decisions without unnecessary and potentially disruptive conflict.

METHODOLOGY

The materials included in this bibliography address the concepts described previously, referring to sources in books, journals, government documents, and monographs. Papers presented at conferences are not included unless they have been published in edited volumes. Mimeographed works are also not included.

These materials focus primarily on literature published between 1975 and 1983, but earlier useful works are also included. Most materials cited are easily accessible through libraries or from the publishers. Each citation provides the reader with necessary information for retrieval. The annotations describe the major theses of the documents.

Materials on community conflict and conflict resolution were collected by several researchers during the past four years, using libraries at the University of Georgia in Athens and Emory University in Atlanta. Additionally, numerous inquiries were made to organizations involved with dispute resolution.

Computer searches of five major bibliographies were conducted in 1981 and again in 1983. These bibliographies reported publications on conflict resolution in education, law, organization theory and development, criminal justice, psychology, social psychology, sociology, and other behavioral sciences.

FORMAT

This bibliography should prove valuable to anyone interested in community conflict. These people could be administrators and government officials operating programs and providing services, citizens involved in dispute resolution in their homes and communities, academicians conducting research in the field of conflict resolution, and many others.

Thus, including major works from a number of fields was thought to be essential. When we consider all the possible kinds of disputes in which these individuals might be involved, it is apparent there exists a large amount of material of possible interest. We developed matrices, or grids, to facilitate using the material.

We used a three-way matrix to organize the literature. It features three categories: <u>level of conflict</u>, <u>focus of analysis</u>, and <u>issue area</u>. A description of each category follows. Each publication is listed by number in the matrix in each appropriate cell. One publication could be included in several cells. The publications are alphabetically listed and numbered by author.

A. <u>Level of Conflict</u>

In this matrix, publications are catalogued according to the level of the conflict. Included are:

1. <u>interpersonal</u>, or disputes between two persons;

2. <u>group</u>, or disputes among group members;

3. <u>organizational</u>, or disputes between groups in an organization, <u>role conflicts</u>, or hierarchical conflicts, including labor/management disputes;

4. <u>community</u>, or disputes between organizations or institutions, or system-wide disputes.

B. <u>Focus of Analysis</u>

In this scale, publications are organized based on the focus of the analysis of the publication. The categories are:

1. <u>Conflict theory and development</u>: publications that analyze the conflict or dispute resolution process and that suggest ways to resolve the conflict; subheadings are provided in Table 1 only, described in the following:

    a. Conflict theory: theoretical works on what conflict is, how it can be resolved, and the dynamics of the process itself.
    b. "How-to" works: publications which give directions to the reader on improving personal and managerial skillls in managing conflict.

2. <u>Models</u>: conceptual ways to understand conflict, and its resolution are proposed;

3. <u>Laboratory Experiments</u>: publications reporting activities in which theories were tested under experimental or laboratory conditions;

many social psychology articles will be included in this category. (Table I only)

    4.   Field Studies: case studies and reports of applications of behavioral technology to resolve conflict

    5.   Ethics: publications dealing with the ethics of intervention, conflict resolution strategies, and other normative issues.

C. Issue Area:

In this scale, the type of organization or structure in which the conflict is described is the basis for the categorization. The areas included are:

    1.   Family: disputes affecting couples, children, marriage and divorce;

    2.   Education: publications involving institutions of higher education; public schools, etc.;

    3.   Community: publications about conflicts and/or programs in community organizations and groups;

    4.   Judicial: publications about programs operating in conjunction with, or serving as alternatives to, the courts;

    5.   Environmental: a fairly new and complex area, it includes literature on environmental mediation, involving simultaneous disputes among many individuals, groups, and organizations regarding the conflict among protection, preservation and utilization of natural resources.

ABOUT THE TABLES:

Articles are located, by number, in appropriate boxes in the three tables.

    Table I: Horizontal axis: Level of conflict
                    Vertical axis: Focus of publication

    Table II: Horizontal axis: Level of conflict
                    Vertical axis: Issue area

    Table III: Horizontal axis: Focus of publication
                    Vertical axis: Issue area

TABLE
LEVEL OF CONFLICT

Focus of Publication	Interpersonal Conflict	Group Conflict	Organizational Conflict	Interorganizational Conflict
Conflict Theory and Development	8 49 123 11 54 125 29 61 147 36 63 149 37 67 38 71 39 74 40 91 41 120	3 49 96 8 54 97 11 56 125 24 61 131 29 67 140 33 71 152 39 74 154 40 91 41 92	3 41 75 113 8 43 77 114 11 49 80 122 22 54 89 131 26 56 91 132 28 61 93 147 29 65 96 152 39 71 97 40 74 112	3 49 104 8 54 121 11 61 123 26 66 127 27 67 131 29 71 144 33 74 39 77 42 91
"How-to" Publications	40 150 60 67 91 110 115 147 149	40 154 60 67 92 110 115 149 150	7 60 91 94 110 115 122	60 115
Models	8 72 11 93 21 120 36 141 37 142 40 144 63 145	11 92 145 13 93 30 97 36 98 40 141 65 142 91 144	3 89 141 11 93 144 30 96 151 36 97 40 98 43 112 81 114	11 141 30 144 33 151 36 40 66 98
Laboratory Experiments	70 73 86 128	48 50 70 86 136	18 48 50	
Field Studies	32 146	12 13 17 138 146	5 55 12 59 13 75 15 81 17 130	6 17 130
Ethics	7 146 11 148 34 37 41 67	7 148 8 11 34 37 67	7 75 11 87 34 109 37 148 41 67	7 109 11 148 26 34 37 67

TABLE II

LEVEL OF CONFLICT

Issue Area	Interpersonal Conflict	Group Conflict	Organizational Conflict	Interorganizational Conflict
Family	25 31 35 57 62 84 124	35 57 124	57 100	57
Education	9 76	9 76 156	9 10 76 100 129 156	9
Community	31 46 80 107	5 27 38 46 58 68 80 107	5 80 6 82 7 107 27 139 33 38 46 53	5 80 6 107 7 108 33 116 38 119 53 134 71 139 79
Judicial	1 2 3 32 90	1 2 4 18 32	1 2 18 32 82	1 2 18 32 82
Environmental	53 137	53 137	53 137	53 80 137 139

5B

TABLE III
FOCUS OF PUBLICATION

Issue Area	Conflict Theory and Development	Models	Field Studies	Ethics
Family	20 57 62 64 78	25 64 78 90 124	4 19 31 35 57 84 85 88	7
Education	9 10 99 111 133 143 156	9 10	116 117 119 129 133	7 9
Community	33 72 38 95 46 107 47 108 57 134 58 135 69 153 71 155	1 79 5 107 9 126 38 135 58 71 72 78	2 46 83 118 4 51 88 119 5 52 100 134 6 53 103 135 16 58 105 139 31 68 106 155 38 79 107 45 82 116	1 7 83 107 108
Judicial	32 47 69 101 102 108	32 69 78	14 68 16 82 18 102 19 103 32 139 35 52 53	7 32 34 69
Environmental	137		53	7

5C

ANNOTATIONS

1. Abel, R.L. 1973. "A comparative theory of dispute institutions in society." Law and Society Review 8(2):217-347.

    In this article, the author proposes norms that support a social theory of law, as distinguished from the law or jurisprudence, and describes a "model for the analysis of dispute institutions in society." Abel reports a cross-cultural study of dispute institutions and recommends dispute institutions as agents for social change. Also provided is an extensive bibliography.

2. Alper, B.S. and Nichols, L.T. 1981. Beyond the Courtroom: Programs in community justice and conflict resolution. Lexington, Mass.: Lexington Books/D.C. Heath.

    The authors describe five dispute resolution programs: mediation, arbitration, restitution, victim assistance and compensation, and citizen panels. Communities are increasingly turning to these programs as alternatives to dispute resolution in the courts. The authors compare the growth of the community dispute programs to the growth of citizen involvement in other areas of the community that has resulted in the organization of self-help groups, cooperatives, and neighborhood health centers, as well as an increased concern for the quality of community schools.
    The authors organize and present literature on community justice programs in the United States and in other parts of the world, and then describe a number of these programs. They have also included an extensive bibliography and a national directory of conflict resolution programs.

3. Bacharach, S.B. and Lawler, E.J. 1980. Power and Politics in Organizations: The social psychology of conflict, coalitions, and bargaining. San Francisco: Jossey-Bass.

    The authors propose a model, called a "paradigm of intra-organizational politics," in which the social psychology of politics is integrated with a structural analysis of organizations. They outline 103 hypotheses, or propositions, in this model.
    Practitioners should be particularly interested in the introductory chapter and chapters 6-8 on conflict among coalitions as a form of bargaining. The conclusion summarizes the premises of the work and also proposes applications of the bargaining model in the fields of organizational analysis and collective bargaining.

4. Bard, M. 1980. "Functions of the police and the justice system in family violence." In Violence and the Family, edited by M.R. Green. Boulder, Colo.: Westview Press.

    The author presents the results of three studies that assessed the impact of conflict resolution training on law enforcement officers and their handling of domestic disputes.

5. Benjamin, A.J. and Levi, A.M. 1979. "Process minefields in intergroup conflict resolution: The Sdot Yam workshop." *Journal of Applied Behavioral Science* 15(4):507-519.

   In this article, the authors report a study of a two-day workshop in which Arabs and Jews in Israel developed a proposal for peace in the Middle East. The findings of the study indicate that there are two simultaneous activities to be observed in any conflict, task and process, and that it may be helpful to assign two consultants to monitor both activities. Presented is a model that was used in the design of the workshop.

6. Berlew, D.E. and LeClere, W.E. 1974. "Social intervention in Curacao: A case study." *Journal of Applied Behavioral Science* 10(1):29-52.

   The authors report the results of a project in which a two-part program, motivation training for residents and leadership training, was initiated on the island of Curacao. Prior to the program's initiation, there had been incidents of violence and conflict between island residents and leaders. The implications of the program are discussed as well.

7. Bermant, G.; Kelman, H.C.; and Warwick, D.P. 1978. *The Ethics of Social Intervention*. Washington, D.C.: Hemisphere Publishing Corp.

   This book is the outgrowth of papers presented at a 1973 conference sponsored by the Battelle Seattle Research Center. The conference focused on the ethics of social intervention as applied in behavior modification, encounter groups, organization development, education, and resolution of community disputes, as well as income maintenance, federal housing, and family planning programs.
   The section dealing with community dispute resolution should be of special interest to policy makers and implementers. Written by James Laue and Gerald Cormick, this section discusses five roles an intervenor may play in a dispute--activist, advocate, mediator, researcher, and enforcer. Using a case study, the authors discuss the requisite skills for each role and outline the ethical implications for this growing field of community conflict resolution. In addition, they propose core values of freedom, justice, and empowerment and suggest that dispute settlement cannot be acceptable if these values are violated.

8. Bernard, J. 1965. "Some current conceptualizations in the field of conflict." *American Journal of Sociology* 70(4):442-454.

   This article provides an overview of the theoretical approaches used to date to study conflict. The review spans a number of disciplines and approaches, including game theory, economic models, and international conflict, and discusses the strengths and weaknesses of each approach.
   For those interested in information about the bases of current conceptions of factors influencing conflict, this is a valuable review.

9. Birnbaum, R. 1980. "Constructive conflict in academic bargaining." In *New Directions for Higher Education (Resolving Conflict in Higher Education) no. 32* 8(4): 69-79.

The author proposes three ideas: 1) that an understanding of intergroup conflict can be useful in understanding behaviors; 2) that it is possible to analyze bargaining processes to determine whether they are constructive or destructive; and 3) that it is possible to change those processes. The author suggests particular ways to change the problem-solving approach to produce more effective solutions.

10. Birnbaum, R. 1980. *Creative Academic Bargaining: Managing conflict in the unionized college and university.* New York: Columbia University, Teachers College Press.

As more of the public sector is unionized, the need for the application of alternative methods to resolve conflicts will grow. This book addresses destructive and constructive factors in the bargaining process and suggests "creative academic bargaining" as a way to make this process constructive. Methods of managing conflict are described, as well as strategies to increase problem-solving potential. The author suggests that third-party intervenors should be used in a variety of capacities and describes ways to select participants for the bargaining process.

11. Blake, R.R. and Mouton, J.S. 1970. "The fifth achievement." *Journal of Applied Behavioral Science* 6(4):413-426.

The authors assert that there have traditionally been four channels to follow in managing differences between individuals: the scientific method, politics, law and the police powers of the law, and organizational hierarchy. However, the authors suggest that in a truly advanced problem-solving society these methods are not sufficient--each individual needs to understand the causes of conflict and to learn the skills to resolve conflict. They present a conflict grid which describes individuals' reactions to a conflict and the motivations governing their actions. The concern of these individuals for people and for production of results is measured on the grid.

12. Blake, R.R.; Mouton, J.S.; and Sloma, R.L. 1965. "The union-management intergroup laboratory: Strategy for resolving intergroup conflict." *Journal of Applied Behavioral Science* 1(1):25-57.

In this publication, the authors report the application of behavioral science technology on conflict between union representatives and management officials. The authors present a situation in which an intergroup laboratory was utilized and then give the results of the experience. The goal of this process is to gain the ability to move from a win-lose environment to a cooperative, problem-solving one.

13. Blake, R.R.; Shepard, H.A.; and Mouton, J.S. 1964. *Managing Intergroup Conflict in Industry*. Houston, Tex.: Gulf Publishing Co.

    Drawing from their experience in organizational consulting and in the academic world, the authors designed this book for professional managers in industry and large organizations. They review several potentially dysfunctional approaches to conflict resolution, including win-lose tactics, bargaining, compromise, withdrawal, and isolationism, and propose a new approach, called *intergroup*, or *mutual*, problem-solving. The authors present several case studies that provide examples of applications of the intergroup approach.

14. Blomberg, T.G. and Caraballo, S.L. 1979. "Accelerated family intervention in juvenile justice: An exploration and a recommendation for constraint." *Crime and Delinquency* 25(4):497-502.

    This article reports the results of legislation in Florida that authorizes the juvenile court to require families of youthful offenders to participate in specialized family counseling and special services. The rationale behind the legislation is to encourage participation in diversionary programs other than the formal court system.

15. Brooks, D.; Winsor, J.; and Shoemaker, T. 1980. "Interpersonal communication and human relations training for corrections personnel." *Communication Education* 29(1):54-60.

    This article reports a case study in which a one-day training program on interpersonal communication was implemented for corrections officers from jails and a state penitentiary.

16. Brown, E.C. 1979. "Evaluation of the Akron 4-A project." In *Resolution of Major Disputes*. Washington, D.C.: U.S. Congress House Subcommittee on Courts, Civil Liberties, and the Administration of Justice.

    This paper reports the results of an evaluation of the Arbitration as an Alternative to Minor Criminal Complaints Program (4-A) in Akron, Ohio. More than 52 percent of the cases from the municipal prosecutor's office were diverted to this program; the program had a high success rate in resolving differences. Also, the 4-A Program proved to be quite cost-effective in minimizing costs to the public.

17. Brown, L.D.; Aram, J.D.; and Bachner, D.J. 1974. "Interorganizational information sharing: A successful intervention that failed." *Journal of Applied Behavioral Science* 10(4):533-554.

    The authors of this article relate the results of an intervention in a conflict between two organizations and review the mixed effects of the third-party intervenor in interorganizational conflict resolution.

18. Bucholz, E. 1980. "The social courts in the German Democratic Republic: Bodies of criminal justice." *International Journal of Comparative and Applied Criminal Justice* 4(1):37-42.

This article explains the function of the social courts in the German Democratic Republic: to serve as "dispute commissions set up in nationally-owned enterprises, residential areas, and agricultural cooperatives." The author has produced a good comparative article.

19. Cantor, I. and Ferguson, P.L. 1976. "From the judge's view--Family counseling in the conciliation court: An alternative to custody litigation." *Conciliation Courts Review* 14(1):1-16.

The authors review a series of cases related to child custody, outlining custody conflicts and other problems that affect the children of divorcing couples. The Custody Counseling Program of the Maricopa County (Calif.) Conciliation Court is described.

20. Chafetz, J.S. 1980. "Conflict resolution in marriage: Toward a theory of spousal strategies and marital dissolution rates." *Journal of Family Issues* 1(3):397-421.

According to the author, spouses may try to use four different strategies in cases of conflict: authority, control, influence, and manipulation. Rates of marital dissolution are a function of the relative equality between spouses in terms of the types of conflict-resolution strategies they can use.

21. Chesler, M.A.; Crowfoot, J.E.; and Bryant, B.I. 1978. "Power training: An alternative path to conflict management." *California Management Review* 21(2):84-90.

The authors review various definitions of conflict and the methods of conflict management these definitions produce.
The authors suggest the need for "power training" that would help "enable other parties to enter the managerial arena, creating mutual access to decision-making and bargaining among political equals." Such access would help powerless people get involved in decisions affecting their lives.

22. Cole, D.L. 1963. *The Quest for Industrial Peace.* New York: McGraw-Hill.

This book is a collection of three lectures given at Harvard University's Business School, Law School, and School of Public Administration. Given by David Cole, former director of the Federal Mediation and Conciliation Service at Harvard University, the lectures covered collective bargaining and the "quest for industrial peace," government's part in labor disputes, and the grievance function in labor relations.

23. Coleman, J.S. 1957. *Community Conflict.* New York: The Free Press.

This book is one of the first to address the sociology of conflict. The tensions highlighted by cases in this classic text became more evident during the 1960s in urban areas and on college campuses throughout the nation. It offers a valuable historic perspective.

24. Collins, B.E. and Guetzkow, H. 1964. *A Social Psychology of Group Processes for Decision-Making*. New York: John Wiley & Sons.

   This is a highly detailed exploration of the factors that can facilitate or impede decision-making within groups. The authors address several concepts involved in group decision-making, including power, information, group size, social motivation, resources, social influence, environmental stimuli, and various types of conflict. They then develop propositions from the literature on small group research that can be adapted for use in larger groups.

25. Coogler, O.J. 1978. *Structured Mediation in Divorce Settlement: A handbook for divorce mediators*. Lexington, Mass.: Lexington Books/D.C. Heath.

   Mediation, the use of a non-directive, neutral third party during negotiation, has not been used widely in the United States as a method of resolving interpersonal disputes. Its application for marital conflict and divorce settlement has gained only a limited acceptance within the last five to ten years.
   This text provides specific guidelines for mediating conflicts that arise out of a need to develop a settlement agreement or to alter an existing agreement. In addition to presenting an alternative means for couples who are divorcing, the book suggests a number of areas for further research.
   Although the primary focus is on divorce mediation, the model presented helps to explain the role of emotion in any conflict resolution. This should alert those in the broader area of community conflict resolution that outcomes of dispute are often determined by an ability to recognize and to deal with emotional elements in almost any confrontation.

26. Coser, L.A. 1956. *The Functions of Social Conflict*. New York: The Free Press.

   In this work, Coser presents his theory that social conflict is "an essential element in group formation and the persistence of group life." Additionally, he proposes that "in loosely structured groups and open societies, conflict may have stabilizing and integrative functions. Further, social conflict in those environments is a mechanism for adjustment of norms adequate to new conditions."

27. Coser, L.A. 1967. *Continuities in the Study of Social Conflict*. New York: The Free Press.

   After reviewing the functions of social conflict (see no. 26), the author analyzes the contributions of Marx and Durkheim to the theory of social conflict, and applies that theory to emerging political systems in new Asian and African nations. This book represents an important contribution to the development of conflict theory.

28. Derr, C.B. 1978. "Managing organizational conflict: Collaboration, bargaining, and power approaches." *California Management Review* 21(2):76-83.

   The author describes three conflict management modes: collaboration, bargaining, and power-play. He then recommends a contingency approach to conflict management.

29. Deutsch, M. 1973. *The Resolution of Conflict: Constructive and destructive processes*. New Haven, Conn.: Yale University Press.

This book consists of a collection of essays and research papers on conflict resolution written by Deutsch, a social psychologist, and his students. They focused on intergroup conflict. Their research reports studies about how conflict resolution is influenced by trust, bargaining, threat, communication, and cooperation. Chapter 13 should be of special interest to the practitioner considering whether to establish a conflict resolution program.

30. Doyle, M. and Straus, D. 1976. *How to Make Meetings Work: The new interaction method*. New York: Wyden Books.

This book is a how-to manual, written particularly for managers. The authors propose a theory, called *facilitation*. Facilitation is only part of the Interaction Method, a method in which the authors report to have trained thousands of organizational representatives.

The authors outline ingredients of an effective meeting and suggest that every meeting needs both structure and leadership--leadership takes precedence over content and process. Participants in every meeting have very definite roles. The leader of the group retains control over the meeting's content, while the meeting facilitator takes responsibility for *process*: i.e., getting all members to contribute to the content and to arrive at a consensus.

31. Driscoll, J.M.; Meyer, R.G.; and Schanie, C.F. 1973. "Training police in family crisis intervention." *Journal of Applied Behavioral Science* 9(1):62-82.

One of the most common circumstances leading to violence in the community involves requests for police assistance in domestic conflicts. This article reports on the results of a training program for police officers in dealing with family disputes.

32. Dubois, P.L., ed. 1982. *The Analysis of Judicial Reform*. Lexington, Mass.: Lexington Books/D.C. Heath.

Originating in a symposium on judicial reform sponsored by the National Institute of Justice and published by the Policy Studies Journal, this volume contains works that analyze research on past, current, and proposed reforms in our judicial system.

33. Duke, J.T. 1976. *Conflict and Power in Social Life*. Provo, Utah: Brigham Young University Press.

The author reviews contributions of major conflict theorists and presents a theory based on power and ideology that incorporates elements of all the reviewed theories.

34. Eckhoff, T. 1967. "The mediator, the judge, and the administrator in conflict-resolution." *Acta Sociologica* 10(3):148-172.

The author distinguishes among the three roles that a third party may assume in conflict resolution, defines their functions, and suggests normative factors to be considered in each role.

35. Edmonton Family Court Conciliation Service. 1978. <u>Edmonton (Canada) Family Court Marriage Conciliation Service: Five-year summary of operations, 1972-1977</u>. Edmonton, Alberta: EFCCS.

This report summarizes the first five years of the Edmonton Family Court Marriage Conciliation Service. At any point in marital legal proceedings, an attorney or judge involved in the case may refer a family to the conciliation service for counseling. The purpose of the service is for the conciliation of any major differences, not necessarily complete conciliation of the marriage.

36. Eiseman, J.W. 1977. "A third-party consultation model for resolving recurring conflicts collaboratively." <u>Journal of Applied Behavioral Science</u> 13(3):303-314.

In this article, the author proposes that conflicts can be resolved collaboratively, and that doing so can be cost-beneficial. The author presents two models using a third-party consultant and suggests times when the method may be used.

37. Eiseman, J.W. 1978. "Reconciling 'incompatible' positions." <u>Journal of Applied Behavioral Science</u> 14(2):133-150.

In this article, the author expands on his conflict resolution theory presented in a previous work. In Eiseman's value-based process, called <u>integrative framework construction</u>, both parties work together to agree upon a mutual solution. Examples of possible applications of this theory are provided.

38. Eldridge, A.F. 1979. <u>Images of Conflict</u>. New York: St. Martin's Press.

This work integrates contributions from the various social sciences with the study of conflict and communication, psychological and perceptual dimensions, and violence. Chapters on racial conflict, political violence, and international conflict include case studies. Bargaining as a strategy in conflict resolution is suggested and then analyzed. The final chapter summarizes the premises of the work and suggests factors that an individual may consider in dealing with conflict.

39. Ferguson, C.K. 1968. "Concerning the nature of human systems and the consultant's role." <u>Journal of Applied Behavioral Science</u> 4(2):179-193.

This article explores the opportunities for competition or collaboration that exist in relationships and explains the role of the consultant in facilitating collaboration.

40. Filley, A.C. 1975. <u>Interpersonal Conflict Resolution</u>. Glenview, Ill.: Scott, Foresman and Co.

With the thesis that "the opposite of conflict is problem-solving," this book is thus aimed at transforming conflicts (between individuals or within groups) to problem-solving experiences that will "make all involved parties feel like winners." The author suggests that conflict is a process composed of six steps: 1) antecedent conditions, 2) perceived conflict, 3) felt conflict, 4) manifest behavior, 5) conflict resolution or suppression, and 6) resolution aftermath.

He outlines three methods for handling conflict: <u>win-lose</u>, <u>lose-lose</u>, and, his preference, <u>win-win</u>. This last method focuses on <u>ends</u>, not alternatives, and uses two processes, <u>consensus</u> and <u>integrative decision making</u> (IDM).

Filley reviews the theoretical background of the problem-solving process. A number of exercises are included in the appendix to illustrate cooperation and problem-solving behaviors.

41. Filley, A.C. 1978. "Some normative issues in conflict management." <u>California Management Review</u> 21(2):61-66.

The author contrasts methods of conflict resolution or management and suggests problem-solving as a preferred method. He notes that "practiced behaviors are self-reinforcing"; therefore, people need opportunities to practice problem-solving behavior.

42. Fink, C.F. 1968. "Some conceptual difficulties in the theory of social conflict." <u>Journal of Conflict Resolution</u> 12(4):412-460.

In this article, the author reviews theories and literature about social conflict from a number of disciplines. He proposes a broad, working definition of social conflict and recommends a multi-disciplinary approach for dealing with conflict. Fink also suggests a theoretical foundation for future study.

43. Fink, S.L.; Beak, J.; and Taddeo, K. 1971. "Organizational crisis and change." <u>Journal of Applied Behavioral Science</u> 7(1):15-37.

This article presents two models for dealing with crisis. Reviewed is a model of individual crisis that was presented in an earlier article. The other is a similar model that illustrates the phases of stress in an organization. Stress affects an organization's different capabilities, including interpersonal relations, intergroup relations, communication, leadership and decision making, problem handling, planning and goal setting, and the organization's structure. The authors also relate ways an organization can grow through crisis.

While the relationship between crisis and conflict may sometimes be distant, a close connection usually exists. This useful article will be particularly helpful to the intervenor.

44. Fisher, R. 1981. <u>Getting to Yes: Negotiating agreement without giving in</u>. Boston: Houghton Mifflin Co.

This brief book presents a model for negotiating conflicts that is applicable to all levels of disagreement. In an easy-to-read, concise format, the book synthesizes the findings of years of research by the Harvard Negotiation Project. The process, "principled negotiation," or "negotiation on the merits," is four-fold: 1) to separate people from the problem; 2) to focus not on positions but on interests; 3) to generate a variety of possibilities before making decisions; and 4) to insist that some objective standard be the basis of the result.

45. Florida Office of the State Courts Administrator. 1979. *Citizen Dispute Settlement Process in Florida: A study of five programs*. Tallahassee: FOSCA.

This government document reports the results of an evaluation of five citizen dispute settlement programs in Florida. By surveying participants in these programs, program officials developed a profile of satisfaction and agreement. Although the survey response rate was fairly low, the results indicate the types of cases in which the citizen dispute settlement process appears to be most applicable.

46. Ford Foundation. 1978. *Mediating Social Conflict: A Ford Foundation report*. New York: Ford Foundation Press.

This report describes the use of third-party intervention in mediating disputes in a number of different cases. The program goals of the Ford Foundation in funding programs in conflict resolution are also elaborated.

47. Ford Foundation. 1978. *New Approaches to Conflict Resolution*. New York: Ford Foundation Press.

This work presents alternatives to traditional judicial methods, methods that could be used by courts and administrative agencies alike, and offers ways to improve the existing judicial system. Arbitration, conciliation, and other methods are also discussed.

48. Frey, R.L., Jr., and Adams, J.S. 1972. "The negotiator's dilemma: Simultaneous in-group and out-group conflict." *Journal of Experimental Social Psychology* 8(4):331-346.

The experiment described in this article expanded the scope of bargaining behavior beyond the one-on-one interaction by making the conflict situation more complex. Used in the experiment was a labor-management bargaining situation.

49. Fuller, L.L. 1971. "Mediation: Its forms and functions." *Southern California Law Review* 44(2):305-309.

In this essay, the author analyzes mediation, using a collective bargaining situation as the context. He indicates other contexts in which mediation would be useful. The potential tension between "rule of law" and mediation is discussed. This article is an excellent overview of mediation from the legal standpoint.

50. Gamson, W.A. 1961. "An experimental test of a theory of coalition formation." *American Sociological Review* 26(4):565-573.

The author reports an experiment that tested a theory of coalition formation. This theory postulated that "any participant will expect others to demand from a coalition a share of the payoff proportional to the amount of resources that they contribute to a coalition." Gamson defines coalition formation as a "step-by-step process where the participants join two at a time."

In the experiment, 120 college fraternity members were divided into 24 five-man groups. They were placed in a hypothetical political convention, where each participant served as chairman. The chairman controlled some votes, but needed a certain number more in order to "win jobs." Participants soon realized the need for creating a coalition.

51. Gamson, W.A. 1966. "Rancorous conflict in community politics." *American Sociological Review* 31(1):71-81.

According to the author, there are two types of conflict: <u>conventional</u> conflict, in which people disagree but do not attribute evil motives to opponents ("bad faith"); and <u>rancorous</u> conflict, in which each opponent believes the other to have violated certain norms.
In the study, 18 New England communities were analyzed on 54 issues to determine which characteristics lead to rancorous conflict.

52. Garofalo, J. and Connelly, K.J. 1980. "Dispute resolution centers, part 1: Major features and processes." *Criminal Justice Abstracts* 12(3):416-439.

The authors report the findings of a study of dispute resolution centers, also called neighborhood justice centers. They describe the common characteristics and features of the centers. They then compare and contrast the centers with court-annexed programs, small claims courts, and groups or organizations that arbitrate civil claims.

53. Goldmann, R.B., ed. 1980. *Roundtable Justice: Case studies in conflict resolution*. Boulder, Colo.: Westview Press.

In this report to the Ford Foundation, the contributors present case studies of conflict resolution in which third-party intervenors were used successfully. The situations they analyze include prison disputes, environmental land use mediation, Indian/land disputes, housing disputes, and desegregation of public schools.

54. Golembiewski, R.T. 1979. *Approaches to Planned Change* (Two volumes): *Part 1: Orienting perspectives and micro-level interventions. Part 2: Macro-level interventions and change-agent strategies*. New York: Marcel Dekker, Inc.

This work is a revised and expanded version of Golembiewski's earlier work, *Renewing Organizations*. In these two new volumes, Golembiewski presents a description of the theory and practice of organization development (OD) based on the laboratory approach. The work considers how individuals and organizations can make more effective choices and cope better with change.
Part 1 addresses the theoretical underpinnings of the OD Laboratory Approach and describes individual and group interventions. Part 2 relates large-organization and system-wide interventions.
Golembiewski suggests that the intervenor may play five roles: facilitative, gatekeeping, diagnostic, architectural, and mobilizing. Additionally, he notes that the three approaches in OD interventions propose very different views of conflict and aggressiveness.
Other areas of note are the discussions of conflicts/crises of agreement and disagreement, and confrontation and team building (in Part 1, pgs. 306 and 318).

55. Golembiewski, R.T.; Tattner, J.B.; and Miller, G.J. 1979. "Designing an arbitration system for a mass transportation construction project." Arbitration Journal 34(3):14-24.

In this case study of the planning of the Metropolitan Atlanta Regional Transportation Authority, the authors relate the background and decisions that resulted in selecting arbitration as the method to use in resolving contract disputes. The expectation was that this method would encourage both the participation of contractors in the program and the federal government's support.
The appendices include contract clauses relating to arbitration and procedures for contractor claims.

56. Goodge, P. 1978. "Intergroup conflict: A rethink." Human Relations 31(6):475-487.

The author notes that there has been little study of intergroup conflict since the 1950s and 1960s, when a significant amount of research was conducted. He takes the position that there is still an inadequate understanding of social conflict and proposes that, contrary to common belief, more than one kind of conflict does exist. This new approach will have implications for the future study of conflict.

57. Green, M.R., ed. 1980. Violence and the Family. Boulder, Colo.: Westview Press.

This text is a collection of papers presented at a symposium at the 1979 American Association for the Advancement of Science. The papers offer a "sociological perspective" on causes of family violence, television's effect on preschool viewers, and ethnopsychiatric dimensions in family violence. Also discussed is how the police function in family violence. [See Bard (no. 4) for discussion of the importance of conflict resolution training for police officers.]

58. Gricar, B.G. and Brown, D.L. 1981. "Conflict, power, and organization in a changing community." Human Relations 34(10): 877-893.

The authors use two theories of conflict and conflict management, the integrative and adversarial, to examine a two-year community conflict that occurred among groups with differing power. They present the theoretical basis of the study. According to the authors, "analysis of the case suggests propositions that link concepts of conflict, organization, and power across both integrative and adversarial theories of conflict."

59. Haizlip, T.M.; Corder, B.F.; and Planavsky, G. 1979. "Hospital-court collaboration in resolving differences over discharges of adolescents." Hospital and Community Psychiatry 30(1):9-13.

The authors discuss a hospital program that was initiated to improve communication between the court and the hospital staff in dealing with adolescent patients. The program was particulary concerned with situations in which adolescents were being discharged by court order without medical recommendation.

60. Hart, L.B. 1981. _Learning from Conflict: A handbook for trainers and group leaders_. Reading, Mass.: Addison-Wesley.

In the introduction to this how-to book, Gordon Lippitt reports on the results of an American Management Association survey of executives, middle managers, and vice presidents. Lippitt reports that 24 percent of the survey respondents spend their time dealing with conflict. However, other professionals, including hospital administrators, mayors and city managers, spend nearly 49 percent of their time in conflict management.

This book is designed to help the reader accept and channel conflict. The author provides exercises and designs for recognizing, diagnosing, and dealing with conflict, and explains how to develop personal skills for handling conflict.

61. Harvey, J.B. 1974. "The Abilene paradox: The management of agreement." _Organizational Dynamics_ 3(1):63-80.

According to the author, the Abilene paradox often occurs when organizations try to deal with problems. The organizations take actions that contradict recommendations made by available data. In so doing, they compound rather than solve their problems.

Harvey believes that organizations make many decisions that contain false assumptions. All participants in the decision-making process have made these false assumptions. As a result, none of the involved parties find the action followed to be agreeable. He offers a humorous story to illustrate this belief.

The author presents three examples of the Abilene paradox and uses several psychological concepts to explain the paradox's logic: action anxiety, negative fantasies, real risk, separation anxiety, fear of conflict, and group think. He recommends solving conflicts by using the direct-confrontation method.

62. Haynes, J.M. 1978. "Divorce mediator: A new role." _Social Work_ 23(1):5-9.

The author suggests that the current adversarial system of our courts produces embittered divorces. Haynes recommends as an alternative that couples seek counseling from a family therapist trained in mediation. According to the author, "in assisting the parties to reach a settlement, the mediator defuses the anger, focuses the rage, and turns them from the past to the future." Haynes also discusses other benefits that divorce mediation will provide to the judiciary and the family. This article considers the subject from the point of view of the social worker, but also addresses effects on the judicial courts system and the families.

63. Heppner, P.P. 1978. "A review of the problem-solving literature and its relationship to the counseling process." _Journal of Counseling Psychology_ 25(5):366-375.

The author uses a problem-solving model developed by D'Zurilla and Goldfried to propose that the field of counseling contains a problem-solving process. A review of literature from several fields is included.

64. Herrman, M.S.; McKenry, P.C.; and Weber, R.E. 1979. "Mediation and arbitration applied to family conflict resolution: The divorce settlement." The Arbitration Journal 34(1):17-21.

The authors describe the traditional adversarial method used in divorces and suggest mediation and arbitration as two alternatives to this method.

65. Hersey, P. and Blanchard, K.H. 1977. Management of Organizational Behavior: Utilizing human resources, 3d ed. Englewood Cliffs, N.J.: Prentice-Hall.

In this text on organizational behavior, the authors devote considerable attention to a model of organizational conflict that is based on the theory suggested by Blake, Shepard, and Mouton (see no. 13). They present a cube that depicts organizational conflict and possible outcomes and behaviors. Types of organizational conflict include win-lose power struggle, third-party intervention, or "fate." Potential outcomes are withdrawal, isolation, or indifference/ignorance. Possible behaviors are problem-solving, compromise/bargaining/mediation, and "smoothing over."

66. Himes, J.S. 1980. Conflict and Conflict Management. Athens: The University of Georgia Press.

According to the author, this book "seeks to summarize and synthesize some...knowledge of both the science of 'social' conflict and the technology of conflict management." Himes integrates existing literature on the sociology of social conflict and proposes a model to explain conflict, applying it to issues of social structure and social power.

67. Hocker-Wilmot, J. and Wilmot, W.W. 1978. Interpersonal Conflict. Dubuque, Iowa: William C. Brown Co.

The authors propose that many traditional beliefs about conflict are dysfunctional; e.g., that "harmony is normal, conflict is abnormal, conflicts and disagreements are synonymous; conflict is pathological; conflict is not a productive use of energy." They propose that conflict be viewed from a communication perspective and provide a new definition of conflict:
"Conflict is an expressed struggle between at least two
  interdependent parties, who perceive incompatible goals,
  scarce rewards, and interference from the other party in
  achieving their goals. They are in a position of opposition
  in conjunction with cooperation."
The authors further suggest that conflict can actually be productive as long as it can be handled (see Coser, nos. 26 and 27). They review styles of individual and relational conflict management.
A chapter is devoted to the importance of understanding power relationships, structures, issue analysis and goal-setting, and tactics and strategies. Perhaps of most interest to community intervenors will be chapter 7, which outlines personal criteria and intervention tactics and suggests ways for an individual to serve as his or her own intervenor.

68. Hofrichter, R. 1980. "Neighborhood justice and the elderly: Policy issues." Washington, D.C.: National Council of Senior Citizens, Criminal Justice and the Elderly Program; U.S. Department of Justice, Law Enforcement Assistance Administration.

Neighborhood justice centers (NJCs) are explored as an alternative way of resolving conflicts in neighborhoods through the use of mediation and conciliation. The author believes that these centers may have particular implications for the elderly.
The author reviews the concept of neighborhood justice centers after having visited a number of centers, particularly those with large proportions of elderly residents. He reports his findings and makes recommendations for the future.

69. Holland, K. 1982. "The twilight of adversariness: Trends in civil justice." In *The Analysis of Judicial Reform*, edited by P.L. Dubois. Lexington, Mass.: Lexington Books/D.C.Heath.

The author describes the traditional model of civil adjudication, originally developed in England and subsequently adopted in the U.S. Based on the use of adversaries, this model has resulted in increased litigation and controlled adjudication. Holland describes a contrasting model, developed in European countries, called the inquisitorial model, that emphasizes negotiation and mediation. He notes that the adversarial system is waning in the U.S. and suggests both positive and negative implications that should be addressed.

70. Houlden, P.; LaTour, S.; Walker, L.; and Thibaut, J. 1978. "Preference for modes of dispute resolution as a function of process and decision control." *Journal of Experimental Social Psychology* 14(1):13-30.

The authors report findings from an experiment in which they tried to assess the relationship of control distributed among participants to the classification of dispute-resolution procedures.

71. Jandt, F.E, ed. 1973. *Conflict Resolution through Communication*. New York: Harper & Row.

According to the author, the text's purpose is to "provide a broader basis for the study of conflict." The book is designed for students in communication and speech classes and in advanced courses in conflict. It can also be used as an interdisciplinary text i several other areas.
Jandt's article on the use of simulations for studying conflict and communication introduces this edited volume, which includes such authors as Blake and Mouton, Deutsch, Doob, and Katz. Types of conflict, from individual to communitywide conflict, are discussed.
Part five, on societal conflict, includes articles on social protest, racial conflict, and civil unrest. An extensive bibliography is also included.

72. Janis, I.L. and Mann, L. 1977. <u>Decision Making: A psychological analysis of conflict, choice, and commitment.</u> New York: The Free Press.

The authors review the literature on conflict from a number of disciplines. They propose a model of conflict to explain coping behaviors of people faced with making decisions under stress. Those involved in community conflict resolution will find the model useful in understanding the types of factors that influence decisions of persons dealing with stressful situations.

Chapter 5 discusses the application of the model to policy-making environments. It should interest practitioners from a variety of fields. Additionally, chapters 13 and 14 suggest further applications in training intervenors.

73. Judd, C.M. 1978. "Cognitive effects of attitude conflict resolution." <u>Journal of Conflict Resolution</u> 22(3):483-498.

The author reports the results of an experiment designed to test the methodology of attitude conflicts. The subjects were male undergraduates at Columbia University. Using role play, the subjects took a position on an issue. Either competition or cooperation was introduced with regard to the position taken by each student and his interaction with other subjects.

The results of the experiment support the hypothesis that competition leads to "a decreased perceived similarity between the positions and an emphasis upon those ways in which the positions differed the most. Cooperation [has the] opposite effects." In other words, the goals are different in cooperation and competition. Judd writes that "perceptions of similarity/dissimilarity will be mediated by conceptual changes."

This study has implications for understanding and resolving interpersonal conflict.

74. Kahn, R.L. and Boulding, E., eds. 1964. <u>Power and Conflict in Organizations.</u> New York: Basic Books.

This edited volume presents selected papers from authors who participated in two seminars in 1960 and 1961, conducted by the Foundation for Research on Human Behavior and the Center for Research on Conflict Resolution. Of particular note is the chapter by Daniel Katz on approaches for managing conflict, in which he reviews traditional methods and proposes changing the institutional, or organizational, structure to <u>reduce</u> (not eliminate) built-in conflict.

Another important chapter focuses on role conflict in organizations. Written by Kahn and Wolfe, it reports results of research conducted in three industrial environments to determine individual reactions to role conflict. This chapter also discusses coping responses, especially those associated with overload--e.g., error, omission, approximation, queuing, and filtering.

Other papers explore group reactions to conflict, and propose a "pure theory of conflict applied to organizations."

75. Kahn, R.L.; Wolfe, D.M.; Quinn, R.P.; Snoek, J.D.; and Rosenthal, R.A. 1964. *Organizational Stress: Studies in role conflict and ambiguity*. New York: John Wiley & Sons.

The authors predict that the rapid growth of technology in our society, along with the growth of large-scale organizations, will continue to produce conflict and ambiguity. They propose that we need to understand these phenomena and how they will affect individuals both within organizations and in other facets of their lives. The authors conducted a "field study of responses to role conflict and ambiguity in six large industrial plants, and a nationwide survey of individual reactions to occupational role conflicts and ambiguities." Chapter 19 summarizes the results of the study and suggests implications for revising organizations to address--not remove--conflict and ambiguity in organizations.

76. Kaye, P., et al. *Core Curriculum in Preventing and Reducing School Violence and Vandalism, Course 4: Interpersonal Relations: Participant guide and reference notebook*. Chevy Chase, Md.: Center for Human Services. Washington, D.C.: U.S. Department of Justice, Law Enforcement Assistance Administration, Office of Juvenile Justice and Delinquency Prevention.

This course is a section of a seven-part curriculum on the subject of school violence and vandalism. Participants engage in seminars, case analyses, and role-playing situations dealing with gangs, victims, and creative conflict resolution.
Community conflict resolution requires specific types of education. The application of this curriculum appears to have a number of uses in today's society.

77. Kerr, C. 1954. "Industrial conflict and its mediation." *American Journal of Sociology* 60(3):230-245.

According to the author, "organized groups, like individuals, may develop four general types of relationships toward one another: they may isolate themselves; they may cooperate, voluntarily or involuntarily; they may compete; or they may enter into conflict." He points out positive aspects of industrial conflict. Additionally, Kerr defines *tactical mediation* and suggests that, though sometimes helpful, it may increase conflict in some situations rather than reduce it. He proposes the use of "strategical" mediation in these situations.

78. Kessler, S. 1977. *Creative Conflict Resolution: Mediation*. Atlanta, Ga.: National Institute for Professional Training.

The author is an experienced professional mediator who presents a model of mediation. Kessler suggests that this model can be applied in a variety of types of disputes (e.g., from business partners attempting to reallocate company resources or goals, to a couple seeking to dissolve a marriage). The model sketches the optimal environment for mediation, then suggests how to structure such an environment and how to move through a mediation. The author also discusses how cooperation, goals, and communication influence the dispute process and outcome. The model is helpful to those developing mediation programs.

79. Kettering Foundation. 1979, 1980, 1981. The Negotiated Investment Strategy.

The following series of productions by the Charles F. Kettering Foundation review the first five years of a pilot project created to coordinate public and private investment in cities. The use of mediation and negotiation in a "bottom-up" strategy, i.e., from the local level to the state and federal level, makes this experiment of interest to both policy makers and implementers.

    1979. Negotiating the City's Future.
These papers describe the background in which the program emerged and discuss the role of various actors, including mayors, state officials, and representatives of the Federal Regional Council in Chicago. The cities of St. Paul, Minnesota; Columbus, Ohio; and Gary, Indiana, were to use a model proposed in an article by Coke and Moore. The article outlines the key requirements of the programs and presents an eight-step process. The process moves from organizing and selecting an impartial mediator to evaluating and monitoring performance.

    1980. The Role of the Chicago Federal Regional Council in the Experimental Application of the Negotiated Investment Strategy: I: Executive Summary II. Lessons from St. Paul, Columbus, and Gary.

Each document summarizes the results of implementing the Negotiated Investment Strategy in the three cities and recommends future programs.

80. Kilmann, R.H. and Thomas, K.W. 1978. "Four perspectives on conflict management: An attributional framework for organizing descriptive and normative theory." Academy of Management Review 3(1):59-68.

This article discusses conflict management diagnosis and intervention strategy for managing conflict. It also proposes an organizational scheme for addressing perspectives on conflict from the literature. An extensive bibliography is provided.

81. Kochan, T.A. and Jick, T. 1978. "The public sector mediation process: A theory and empirical examination." Journal of Conflict Resolution 22(2):209-240.

This paper proposes a theory of mediation that is practiced in the public sector. Special sections focus on labor-management relations. The authors present a model that tests hypotheses of possible determinants of mediation effectiveness: settlement or no settlement; proportion of issues open at the outset of mediation that are resolved during mediation; measure of movement off positions held at the outset of mediation; and holding back on concessions. The paper discusses the impact of 1) alternative sources of impasse, 2) situational characteristics, 3) strategies of the mediators, and 4) personal characteristics of the mediators on these determinants.

Findings indicate that differences were related to size of the city in which the conflict occurred. The nature of the impasse procedure did not have the most impact on the effectiveness of the mediation process. This article should be of interest to practitioners, and to researchers as well.

82. Kochan, T.A., et al. 1979. <u>Dispute Resolution under Fact-Finding and Arbitration</u>. New York: American Arbitration Association.

The authors report the results of a study of arbitration and collective bargaining in the public sector. They recommend fact-finding and impasse procedures as alternatives to strikes in the resolution of disputes in public organizations.

The State of New York passed in 1967 legislation that changed the method of dispute resolution for public employees from fact-finding to arbitration. This method has served as a general model for other states, and more than 37 of them have adopted it during the past 10 years. The study compares situations of police and firefighters with New York State teachers. It also compares police and fire fighter negotiations in Wisconsin, Michigan, and Massachusetts with similar negotiations in New York.

83. Kraybill, R.S. 1981. <u>Repairing the Breach</u>: <u>Ministering in community conflict</u>. Scottdale, Penn.: Herald Press.

This manual, published by the director of the Mennonite Conciliation Service, is designed to assist ministers in peacemaking. It includes case studies that highlight theoretical constructs on inter-group, individual, and intra-group conflict. The manual also discusses such conciliation programs as the Mennonite Conciliation Service, the Jewish Conciliation Board, dispute settlement centers, and the victim-offender reconciliation program initiated by the Mennonite Central Committee.

This book provides an excellent summary of community peacemaking.

84. Kressel, K. and Deutsch, M. 1977. "Divorce therapy: An in-depth survey of therapists' views." <u>Family Process</u> 16(4):413-443.

The authors interviewed 21 divorce therapists and addressed three major questions: 1) What criteria distinguish <u>constructive and destructive</u> divorces? 2) What obstacles impede a constructive divorce? and 3) What strategies and tactics of therapeutic intervention are most useful, and how can they be classified?

Respondents were living primarily in the New York/Boston area, serving a fairly elite clientele, and conducting approximately 20 percent of their practice as divorce therapists.

The authors identified four stages of psychic divorce: the pre-divorce decision period, the decision period, the period of mourning, and the period of recovery. They determined the criteria of a constructive divorce: a complete psychological separation between the divorced couple, a minimum of emotional injury to children, a resulting personal growth for both parties, and no feelings of failure and self-disparagement.

Divorce therapists stated that their two objectives in counseling divorcing couples were to help their clients decide whether to divorce and then to assist the couple in negotiating an agreement. The three types of strategies used are: 1) reflexive, which primarily affects the therapist; 2) contextual, in which the therapist attempts to affect the climate of the dispute by introducing and requiring ground rules; and 3) substantive, in which the therapist is actively involved in developing and implementing agreements.

The field of divorce therapy and divorce settlement mediation is relatively new. At the time of this article's publication, there were no training programs specifically for divorce therapy, nor were there any public agencies conducting divorce mediation programs. Family conciliation courts came closest to providing this service.

85. Kressel, K., et al. 1977. "Mediated negotiations in divorce and labor disputes: A comparison." Conciliation Courts Review 15(2):9-12.

The current adversary system of the courts pits lawyer against lawyer. In this article, the authors propose an alternative: that a neutral third party implement mediation in divorce cases. They report the preliminary findings of a study of nine mediated divorces, in which participants used procedures developed by O.J. Coogler of the Family Mediation Center in Atlanta. The procedure features conjoint sessions held in the presence of the couple, a mediator, and an impartial legal consultant.

The authors discuss four obstacles blocking effective mediation: 1) high levels of internal conflict; 2) scarcity of divisible resource;, 3) naive negotiators; and 4) discrepancy in relative power. They recommend the following as possible solutions to these obstacles: 1) a pre-mediation course in divorce negotiations; 2) an "advocacy" model of mediation; and 3) the handling of emotional issues outside of mediating sessions.

86. Lacy, W.B. 1978. "Assumptions of human nature, and initial expectations and behavior as mediators of sex effects in Prisoner's Dilemma research." Journal of Conflict Resolution 22(2):269-281.

The author reports an experiment that investigated the "influence of assumptions regarding human nature, expectations of opponent's initial behavior, and early game interpersonal behavior on subsequent levels of cooperation in a mixed motive, nonzero sum game." The experiment tested the hypothesis that behavior of males and females would differ based on these criteria.

The experiment's 236 subjects were male and female undergraduate sociology students at the University of Kentucky. The results of the experiment indicate that, although the women held a more positive view of human nature, this view did not affect their expectations of their partner's behavior nor their own initial actions. The women did, however, expect more cooperation from their co-player and therefore they cooperated more. The conclusion was that a female is more likely to base her behavior on her own previous behavior, while a male is likely to base his behavior on his opponent's behavior.

87. Landis, B.I. 1977. Value Judgments in Arbitration: A case study of Saul Wallen. Ithaca, N.Y.: New York State School of Industrial and Labor Relations, Cornell University.

The author relates a brief history of the role of arbitration in labor dispute resolution, focusing on the experiences of Saul Wallen, a full-time labor abitrator and mediator. Wallen is an important figure in the field of labor arbitration because of his long involvement in it and the many contributions he has made. He provides an excellent example of a person who consistently applied personal integrity and high values to labor dispute arbitration. From the beginning of his career in 1946 until its end in 1968, Wallen conducted 6,200 arbitrations.

88. Levens, B.R. and Dutton, D.G. 1980. "Social service role of police: Domestic crisis intervention." Vancouver, B.C., Canada: United Way of Greater Vancouver.

This report reviews programs in Canada designed to train police in domestic crisis intervention. The authors identify components of successful intervention strategies and examine the effects of this training on the Canadian police. They note that the police officers spent more than half their time on social service activities, including family disputes. This fact underscores the need of each officer to use skills such as mediation in the daily exercise of his/her profession.

89. Levin, E. and De Santis, D.V. 1978. <u>Mediation: An annotated bibliography</u>. Ithaca, N.Y.: New York State School of Industrial and Labor Relations, Cornell University.

The authors present an annotated bibliography on mediation, using literature published primarily between 1964 and 1976. They emphasize publications that report on new developments in the field of industrial mediation, including mediation-arbitration and the growing role of collective bargaining in the public sector.

90. Lightman, E.S. and Irving, H.H. 1976. "Conciliation and arbitration in family disputes." <u>Conciliation Courts Review</u> 14(2):12-21.

The article presents a model for dispute resolution in divorce cases involving children. Two elements included are: 1) a system of conciliation as a precondition to any court-sanctioned divorce or separation proceedings; and 2) the availability of arbitration as an alternative to the courts, should the parties be unable to resolve their differences at the conciliation state. The authors note that arbitration may be either binding or advisory and that conciliation should focus on the welfare of the child. A second model is also suggested in which the arbitrator and conciliator are the same.
With the high rate of divorce, and the growing number of children being raised by single parents, alternatives to traditional litigation--like the one offered here--are becoming increasingly important.

91. Likert, R. and Likert, J.G. 1976. <u>New Ways of Managing Conflict</u>. New York: McGraw-Hill.

This book introduces a model for dealing with conflict at all levels. The model is based on organizational theory and management and "System 4." System 4 is a process that includes linking pins and the linking process; leadership styles and values; and win-win problem solving and supportive goal setting. The authors suggest ways to implement System 4 and report two studies of contrasting systems.

92. Likert, R. and Likert, J.G. 1978. "A method for coping with conflict in problem-solving groups." <u>Group and Organization Studies</u> 3(4):427-434.

The authors suggest that the problem-solving method in groups may at times lead to conflict among group members and may result in a win-lose solutions. They recommend adding another step before group members discuss possible solutions. After first stating the problem, group members should list conditions that solutions must meet.

93. Lippitt, G.L. 1982. "Managing conflict in today's organizations." *Training and Development Journal* 36(7):66-74.

The article emphasizes the importance of conflict management as a skill for managers in organizations, as illustrated in a recent American Management Association survey. The premise is that "conflict is an absolutely predictable social phenomenon," one that should be channeled to useful purposes. The article presents a model of five conflict management styles: competing, avoiding, compromising, accommodating, and collaborating. Lippitt also suggests ways to manage conflicts.

94. Loevi, F.J., Jr., and Kaplan, R.P. 1982. *Arbitration and the Federal Sector Advocate: A practical guide*, 2d ed. New York: American Arbitration Association.

The authors present a "how-to" text for advocates involved in federal sector grievance arbitration under the 1978 Civil Service Reform Act.

95. Long, N.E. 1969. "The local community as an ecology of games." In *Urban Government: A reader in administration and politics*, edited by E.C. Banfield. New York: The Free Press.

This article presents a theoretical discussion of the comparability between conflict strategies implied in experimental games research and the various actors or elements representing sources of conflict within a community. Most of the publication's research was conducted before the development of several alternative mechanisms for community conflict resolution. Even so, the materials provide an insightful and necessary bridge between two disparate literatures.

96. Maggiolo, W.A. 1971. *Techniques of Mediation in Labor Disputes*. Dobbs Ferry, N.Y.: Oceana Publications.

This book focuses on mediation in the settling of labor disputes and also discusses the basic concepts of mediation. The author distinguishes between various types of third-party intervention and discusses key elements of successful mediation. These elements include knowing when to intervene, promoting confidentiality, and developing agreements.

97. March, J.G. and Simon, H.A. 1958. *Organizations*. New York: John Wiley & Sons.

March and Simon review literature from a number of disciplines and propose a series of hypotheses about what organizations are and how they function. Of most interest to practitioners and academicians will be chapter five. According to the authors, conflict is "a breakdown in the standard mechanisms of decision-making so that an individual or group experiences difficulty in selecting an action alternative...when an individual or group experiences a decision problem."
They list the three classes of conflict as individual, organizational (individual or group conflict within an organization), and interorganizational. The organization's reactions to conflict include problem-solving, persuasion, bargaining, and politics. The authors review game theory and coalition-building as well. This book contributes to theories in group dynamics, organizational behavior, and public administration.

98. Mastenbroek, W.F.G. 1980. "Negotiating: A conceptual model." Group and Organization Studies 5(3):324-339.

The author proposes a model based on two perspectives: 1) negotiating as a set of dilemmas and 2) negotiating as a combination of four kinds of activities, each connected to a different intention. The dilemmas classify ways of interaction along a continuum, from cooperation to negotiation to fighting. The activities include: 1) distributing benefits and burdens; 2) influencing personal relations and the negotiating climate between the parties; 3) influencing the negotiator's own constituency; and 4) influencing the balance of power between the parties.

99. McCarthy, J.E. 1980. "Conflict and mediation in the academy." New Directions for Higher Education no. 32 (Resolving conflict in higher education) 8(4):1-8.

This article distinguishes mediation from arbitration. It both describes the functions of the mediator and identifies the barriers to and elements of effective mediation. The article also describes the role of the Center for Mediation in Higher Education at the American Arbitration Association.
Practitioners from many disciplines should benefit from this description of mediation.

100. McCoy, S. and Glazzard, P. 1978. "Winning the case but losing the child: Interdisciplinary experiences with PL 94-142." Journal of Clinical Child Psychology 7(3):205-208.

New legislation requires public institutions to provide increasing services to previously unserved members of the population: handicapped children. This legislation increases both the potential for conflict and the need to develop new ways of cooperation. The authors describe the development of a mediation program designed to resolve conflict between parents of handicapped children and school personnel. They focus on how Kansas City is implementing the law by using a multidisciplinary team from Kansas University Medical Center to assist children and to resolve conflict.

101. McEwen, C.A. and Maiman, R.J. 1982. "Mediation and arbitration: Their problems and performance as alternatives to court." In The Analysis of Judicial Reform, edited by P.L. Dubois. Lexington, Mass.: Lexington Books/D.C. Heath.

The authors review previous research in mediation and arbitration to determine whether mediation and arbitration programs are meeting assumed major policy objectives. These objectives include reduced costs and improved access to courts through reduced case loads. Other goals are to influence public perceptions of the process and to increase the quality of justice received by participants. The article outlines issues that still need to be addressed in implementing such programs.

102. McGillis, D. 1980. Neighborhood Justice Centers. Cambridge, Mass.: ABT Associates, Inc.; Washington, D.C.: U.S. Department of Justice, National Institute of Justice.

According to the author, this policy brief describes programs for resolving minor disputes without arrest or formal court action. These programs use conciliation, mediation, or arbitration techniques to deal with interpersonal conflicts. The neighborhood justice center shows much promise as an alternative dispute mechanism to the court system. The court system is costly, overloaded with both civil and criminal cases, and perhaps inaccessible to citizens. The book includes a description of the program as well as information about how to begin a program and how to obtain funding.

103. McGillis, D. 1980. "Neighborhood justice centers as mechanisms for dispute resolution." In New Directions of Psycholegal Research, edited by P.D. Lipsett and B.D. Sales. New York: Van Nostrum Reinhold.

The author reports an analysis of six neighborhood justice centers in cities throughout the United States. Results indicate that between 80 and 95 percent of the cases end in permanent dispute resolution. The cases handled are family matters, neighborhood conflicts, bad check charges (for which restitution is arranged), and landlord-tenant cases. The study findings indicate that these centers offer positive alternatives to the traditional court system for permanently resolving many disputes now handled by the courts.

104. McNeil, E.B., ed. 1965. The Nature of Human Conflict. Englewood Cliffs, N.J.: Prentice-Hall.

This edited volume presents a systematic account of social science and war. Among the contributors to the work are economists, political scientists, psychologists, sociologists, game theorists, and decision theorists. Their common thesis is that a unified understanding of the nature of conflict will result in worldwide peace. They urge all social scientists to work together toward this goal.

105. Merry, S.E. 1979. "Going to court: Strategies of dispute management in an American urban neighborhood." Law and Society Review 13(4):891-925.

This article is an analysis of dispute resolution strategies used by residents of a multi-ethnic neighborhood in an American city. The results emphasize the need to provide alternatives to the formal process of litigation. The legal process represents for these residents one way of resolving interpersonal and crime-related disputes. However, the legal machinery often is not effective in settling such disputes. Without effective conflict resolution, the outcome is frequently violence, avoidance, or even tolerance of ongoing conflict.

106. Metropolitan Human Relations Commission. 1979. Portland (Oregon): Neighborhood mediation pilot project annual research report, 1979. Portland, Oreg.: MHRC.

This document deals with 68 neighborhoods that were served by three mediation centers. It describes and analyzes the activities of this community-based neighborhood mediation project during a one-year period.

107. Nader, L. and Todd, H.F., Jr., eds. 1978. The Disputing Process: Law in ten societies. New York: Columbia University Press.

This edited volume analyzes the ways in which 10 different societies handle disputes. It shows the societal influences of the various cultures. The book also discusses the impact of levels of law on dispute resolution and considers different uses of third-party intervention. It represents an interesting study of the cultural differences of conflict resolution.

108. Parnell, P. 1981. "Community justice versus crime control." In Race, Crime, and Criminal Justice, edited by R.L. McNeely and C.C. Pope. Beverly Hills, Calif.: Sage Publications.

Parnell first reviews the research of a number of cultural anthropologists, including Laura Nader (see no. 107) Nader has studied minorities, their social networks, and their community norms. Parnell proposes using mediation as an alternative to the traditional bureaucratic legal system to resolve community disputes.

109. Payne, S.L. 1980. "Organization ethics and antecedents to social control processes." Academy of Management Review 5(3):409-414.

The author proposes developing a theory of ethics for the behavioral sciences. He reviews some theoretical roots of this field that are based on small-group research on deviance and social control. He then suggests combining current research on business ethics with social science theories.

110. Pneuman, R.W. and Bruehl, M.E. 1982. Managing Conflict: A complete process-centered handbook. Englewood Cliffs, N.J.: Prentice-Hall.

The authors of this brief handbook present how-to information on conflict: how to understand it, identify it, deal with it, and manage it. They propose and explain a problem-solving process called the "interactional process." The final chapter presents a summary of seven critical checkpoints in the conflict management process.

111. Podemski, R.S. and Steele, R. 1981. "Avoid the pitfalls of citizen committees." American School Board Journal 168(4):40-42.

The authors outline some common problems that occur when boards and administrators work with citizen committees. They then suggest possible solutions to these problems.

112. Pondy, L.R. 1967. "Organizational conflict: Concepts and models." Administrative Science Quarterly 12(2):296-320.

The author presents three models of conflict and then proposes a model of the five stages of the "conflict episode." The three models of organizational conflict are bargaining, bureaucratic, and systems, which Pondy combines to elaborate a general theory of conflict.

113. Pondy, L.R.; Fitzgibbons, D.E.; and Wagner, J.A. 1980. Organizational Power and Conflict: A bibliography. Monticello, Ill.: Vance Bibliographies.

   This bibliography provides more than 200 citations related to power and conflict in organizations. The sources are predominantly from sociological and organization theory literature.

114. Pruitt, D.G. 1981. Negotiation Behavior. New York: Academic Press.

   The author describes negotiation as a specific form of decision-making and reviews recent research in the field of negotiating. Pruitt proposes the strategic choice model of negotiation and the goal-expectation hypothesis. Chapters 4-6 explain the theoretical underpinnings of negotiation, and chapter 7 describes third-party interventions.

115. Raiffa, H. 1982. The Art and Science of Negotiation. Cambridge, Mass.: The Belknap Press of Harvard University Press.

   The author presents a view of negotiation with the intent of helping practitioners understand the dynamics of negotiation, improve their interpersonal skills, and look for environmental factors that may affect successful negotiation. The author includes real and hypothetical case studies to illustrate complex negotiations involving several parties and issues.

116. Reichman, M. 1980. "Resolving campus-community conflicts." New Directions for Institutional Advancements, (Effective Community Relations) 10(2):79-92.

   The author relates three case studies involving conflicts between institutions of higher education and local communities. Similarities in the three situations are suggested.

117. Reisman, J. 1982. "Technocracy or politics? Conflict management behavior in public managerial professions." Eugene, Oreg.: Center for Educational Policy and Management, College of Education, University of Oregon.

   This study compares behaviors for handling conflict shown by city managers and school superintendents in Chicago and San Francisco. The findings of the study indicate that each professional handles conflicts differently.

118. Rich, R.C. and Rosenbaum, W.A., eds. 1981. "Citizen participation in public policy." Journal of Applied Behavioral Science 17(4):437-614.

   This issue contains a number of articles relating to citizen involvement in activities of government programs and agencies. While all the articles may interest the administrator, most relevant to community conflict resolution is the article by Rosener, Godschalk, and Stiftel regarding participation in state water planning programs.

119. Rifkin, J., et al. 1980. "Legal studies and mediation." In New Directions for Higher Education no. 32 (Resolving conflict in higher education) 8(4):49-54.

The authors describe a new legal studies program at the University of Massachusetts at Amherst. This program is designed to involve students in nonadversarial dispute resolution and to train them in mediation techniques.

120. Roark, A.E. and Wilkinson, L. 1979. "Approaches to conflict management." Group and Organization Studies 4(4):440-452.

The authors review popular models now used for managing conflict. These include Rogers' client-centered therapy for interpersonal conflicts and a model developed by Levi and Benjamin. Included in the article is an extensive bibliography.

121. Robbins, S.P. 1978. "'Conflict management' and 'conflict resolution' are not synonymous terms." California Management Review 21(2):67-75.

The author distinguishes three stages of thought in the study of conflict--traditionalist, behavioralist, and interactionist. Robbins suggests that conflict varies on a continuum, from no conflict to violence and bloodshed. He identifies differences between functional and dysfunctional conflicts. In addition, he suggests when and how to stimulate conflict and encourages a contingency approach to conflict management.

122. Robbins, S.P. 1974. Managing Organizational Conflict: A non-traditional approach. Englewood Cliffs, N.J.: Prentice-Hall.

With information for both the practitioner and the theorist, this book is particularly useful for managers in all types of organizations. The author encourages an "interactionist" approach to conflict management, one that accepts and encourages conflict as a natural element of change. He says that "constructive conflict has been shown to be an absolute necessity for survival of organizational life, and survival is the primary objective of any organization."

123. Rogers, C.R. 1965. "Dealing with psychological tensions." Journal of Applied Behavioral Science 1(1):6-24.

In this article, the author presents a state-of-the-art description of the behavioral sciences and explains how they are addressing problems and conflict at the following levels: intrapersonal, between two individuals, between groups, and in international situations. He suggests methods of resolving conflict at all levels.

124. Rollin, S.A. and Dowd, E.T. 1979. "Conflict resolution: A model for effective marital and family relations." American Journal of Family Therapy 7(1):61-67.

The authors propose a three-step model designed primarily for marriage and family counselors. The model attempts to improve the communication skills among family members.

125. Rubin, J.Z. and Brown, B.R. 1975. *The Social Psychology of Bargaining and Negotiation*. New York: Academic Press.

As noted by the authors, this publication is a survey of literature from social psychology that emphasizes the processes of bargaining and negotiation. Definitions of basic concepts are provided for readers not familiar with the differences of various forms of bargaining relationships. The book also discusses the structural and social psychological factors that directly influence the nature of negotiation and the potential for successful outcomes. This book should be of value to researchers as well as to practitioners.

126. Sayers, S. 1978. *Problem Solving: A five step model--Keys to community development series: 3*. Washington, D.C.: National Institute of Education.

This booklet is a how-to manual on problem-solving that discusses five steps in the process. These are: 1) to focus on the problem, 2) to search for alternatives, 3) to plan for action, 4) to carry out the plan, and 5) to assess the results. This publication's simple, straightforward presentation makes it of interest to many different participants in the process of community dispute resolution.

127. Schlenker, B.R. and Bonoma, T.V. 1978. "Fun and games: The validity of games for the study of conflict." *Journal of Conflict Resolution* 22(1):7-38.

The authors review arguments on the use of games in the study of social conflict. They propose that these arguments should be addressed in terms of internal validity, external validity, and ecological validity.

128. Schlenker, B.R. and Goldman, H.J. 1978. "Cooperators and competitors in conflict: A test of the 'triangle model.'" *Journal of Conflict Resolution* 22(3):393-410.

This paper reports the results of an application of the Kelley and Stahelski "triangle model," which describes the variations in attitudes and actions of different types of people involved in conflict. This and an alternative model are tested using 158 male and female subjects. The subjects were classified as cooperators or noncooperators, and then paired with a cooperative or noncooperative partner. They then participated in a mixed-motive game that had a cooperative or competitive payoff structure.

Results suggest that noncooperators attribute competitive motives to others, mis-identify cooperative opponents, and also tend to be influenced by neither the immediate situation nor the partner. Cooperators, on the other hand, tend to be more flexible and more likely to perceive a variety of motives in opponents.

Their perceptions appear to be more affected by the situation and the partner. The results suggest to practitioners the importance of establishing personality characteristics of protagonists when attempting to structure a mediation environment or to predict outcomes of negotiation. The results also suggest areas for future research.

129. Sebring, R.H. 1978. "Teacher-administrator conflict: Can it be resolved?" NASSP Bulletin 62(415):37-41.

Collective bargaining and its resultant changes in power among teachers and administrators are suggested as contributing to their conflict. Presented is a case study of a workshop designed to address this problem in one school district.

130. Sebring, R. and Duffee, D. 1977. "Who are the real prisoners? A case of win-lose conflict in a state correctional institution." Journal of Applied Behavioral Science 13(1):23-40.

In this case study of an intervention in a state correctional facility, the authors report the consequences of win-lose conflict at both intra-organizational and interorganizational levels. The highly charged political environment of the discussed conflict is also present in most community organizations. This trait makes this experiment's implications important considerations for intervenors.

131. Shea, G.P. 1980. "The study of bargaining and conflict behavior: Broadening the conceptual arena." Journal of Conflict Resolution 24(4):706-741.

The author reviews and analyzes five publications on conflict behavior and bargaining. The publications deal with industrial relations, psychology, and social psychology. Shea suggests a multidisciplinary approach to solving conflict, primarily in the labor-management area but potentially in other fields. Shea identifies two problem areas requiring particular attention: developing an agenda and dealing with new items. He suggests ways to address these areas at the individual, group, and systemic levels of analysis.

132. Simkin, W.E. 1971. Mediation and the Dynamics of Collective Bargaining. Washington, D.C.: Bureau of National Affairs.

This book presents concepts of the bargaining and conflict resolution process from the labor negotiation perspective. Although the materials have a narrow focus, the text clearly discusses key processes of negotiation that are useful to anyone involved in resolving conflict. Also provided is a list of suggested characteristics of effective mediators. Chapter 5 discusses mediation procedures used during a crisis situation.

133. Stamato, L. 1980. "Taking the initiative: Alternatives to government regulation." In New Directions for Higher Education, no.32 (Resolving Conflict in Higher Education 8(4):55-68.

In this publication, the author proposes methods for academic institutions to avoid conflict with government through self-regulation and joint development of performance standards.

134. Steiner, H.M. 1978. Conflict in Urban Transportation: The people against the planners. Lexington, Mass.: Lexington Books/D.C. Heath.

This document is in two parts. The first part concerns case studies concerning freeways, airports, urban rail transport systems, and bus mass transit systems. The second deals with philosophical, economic, political, environmental, and social contexts of the conflict.

135. Steinmann, D.O.; Smith, T.H.; Jurdem, L.G.; and Hammond, K.R. 1977. "Application of social judgment theory in policy formulation: An example." *Journal of Applied Behavioral Science* 13(1):69-88.

The authors propose the Social Judgment Theory, a method for dealing with disputes. They apply this theory and the use of computer graphics procedures in an actual decision-making process with a public board responsible for developing an open-space land acquisition program. In this case, they attempted to develop more acceptable decisions. Other applications are also cited.

136. Stephenson, G.M. and Kniveton, B.K. 1978. "Interpersonal and interparty exchange: An experimental study of the effect of seating position on the outcome of negotiations between teams representing parties in dispute." *Human Relations* 31(6):555-566.

The authors document the results of an experiment that tested the importance of seating arrangements in resolving disputes. The results support the hypothesis that seating arrangements influence the degree of success that negotiating teams have in arguing their cases.

137. Straus, D.B. 1978. "Mediating environmental disputes." *Arbitration Journal* 33(4):5-8.

In this article, the author presents a method for dealing with multiparty disputes and reviews recent activities in the growing field of environmental mediation. Straus discusses process-facilitation mediation and the use of computers in dispute resolution.

138. Stumpf, S.A. 1977. "Using integrators to manage conflict in a research organization." *Journal of Applied Behavioral Science* 13(4):507-517.

The author reports the result of an intervention in the design of work groups. In this governmental research organization, conflict between work groups and within the groups was interfering with productivity and job satisfaction. In each of four groups, one person was appointed to function as integrator.

139. Sviridoff, M. 1980. "Recent trends in resolving interpersonal, community, and environmental disputes." *Arbitration Journal* 35(3):3-9.

The author cites two problems with the existing court system: an overload of cases and the win-lose nature of disputes. He reports examples of alternatives and additions to the formal court process now functioning in New York, Cincinnati, and Detroit. These examples include the American Arbitration Association's mediation and arbitration program, the U.S. government's community relations program, intergovernmental programs, and environmental mediation programs.

140. Swierczek, F.W. 1980. "Collaborative intervention and participation in organizational change." *Group and Organization Studies* 5(4):438-452.

The author reports results of a study of 67 cases of organizational change. He notes that the character of collaboration changes during the intervention's phases of problem determination, goal setting, and solution. Negotiation is the most important factor in problem determination, and mutuality is most important in goal setting. Consensus is most important in the solution phase. The author found little relationship during each phase between collaboration and the perceived effectiveness or the adoption of the change.

141. Thomas, K.W. 1976. "Conflict and conflict management." In *Handbook of Industrial and Organizational Psychology*, edited by M.D. Dunnette. Chicago: Rand McNally.

The author presents two models of conflict based on an extensive review of literature from a number of fields. The models are applicable to conflicts between individuals, groups, or organizations. They deal with process and structure. Thomas suggests diagnostic questions for each model, emphasizes integrative theory development and the need for more complex models, and delineates areas for future research. An extensive bibliography is included.

142. Thomas, K.W. 1978. "Introduction: Conflict and the collaborative ethic." *California Management Review* 21(2):56-60.

In the introduction to this special issue on conflict management, Thomas asserts that the term "conflict management" is replacing conflict resolution. He goes on to discuss the model of conflict intentions, a two-dimensional model with five modes of behavior for handling conflict.

143. Tjosvold, D. 1978. "Cooperation and conflict between administrators and teachers." *Journal of Research and Development in Education* 12(1):138-148.

The role structure of school teachers and administrators is credited with causing much of the conflict between the two groups. The author offers as possible solutions cooperative conflict resolution and collaborative decision making.

144. Twomey, D.F. 1978. "The effects of power properties on conflict resolution." *Academy of Management Review* 3(1):144-150.

The author proposes a model of styles of conflict resolution. He bases the model on two properties of social power: dependency and availability of alternatives. He predicts that these properties determine the method or mode of conflict resolution and influence the resulting behavioral states.

145. Wall, J.A., Jr. 1981. "Mediation: An analysis, review, and proposed research." *Journal of Conflict Resolution* 25(1):157-180.

The author suggests a model of a mediation process. Termed a "paradigm of the negotiated mediation system," the model includes a mediator and two negotiators for the opposing parties. In addition, the article includes reviews of literature on mediation that are organized to illustrate the paradigm. Also offered are future research applications.

146. Walton, R.E. 1968. "Interpersonal confrontation and basic third party functions: A case study." *Journal of Applied Behavioral Science* 4(3):327-344.

In this case study, the author relates the experience of a third-party intervenor involved in helping two directors of interdependent groups in a government agency to confront and to resolve interpersonal and interdepartmental conflict. In addition, the author recommends a number of qualities for an intervenor. This article illustrates the importance of addressing interpersonal problems as well as interdepartmental or intergroup ones.

147. Walton, R.E. 1969. *Interpersonal Peacemaking: Confrontations and third-party consultation.* Reading, Mass.: Addison-Wesley.

The text focuses on interpersonal conflict in large, formal organizations. The author discusses the role of third-party intervenors who are employed either as outside consultants to the organization or as staff within the organization. Also explored is the effectiveness of third-party intervention as it relates to the settling of disputes, the timing of meetings to resolve disputes, the need to state issues, and the role of the third party as advocate and sounding board.

The materials are especially helpful in describing the dynamics of the process of conflict resolution and the frequent need to include a neutral third party to facilitate the resolution process.

148. Walton, R.E. and Warwick, D.P. 1973. "The ethics of organization development." *Journal of Applied Behavioral Science* 9(6):681-698.

Two consultants describe existing issues in the growing field of organization development (OD). They write of "the great potential for good as well as harm in OD" and discuss the three areas in which major ethical dilemmas arise: power, freedom, and professional responsibility.

This is an important article for all potential intervenors, regardless of the level of the intervention.

149. Warehime, R.G. 1980. "Conflict-management training: A cognitive/behavioral approach." *Group and Organization Studies* 5(4):467-476.

The author proposes a conflict-management approach that encourages participants to view and analyze conflict in terms of personal actions and reactions at the cognitive, emotional, and behavioral levels.

At the cognitive level, beliefs and self-conceptions can be identified and changed. At the emotional level, one can learn to remain calm, to think more clearly, and to behave more effectively. At the behavioral level, one can learn to respond to others more effectively and to express oneself more clearly and directly.

It is also possible to respond to the indirect behavior of others. Increased effectiveness in responsive and expressive behaviors can lead to mutual problem solving in situations of conflict. These behaviors can be practiced through role-playing exercises.

150. Warschaw, T.A. 1980. *Winning by Negotiation*. New York: McGraw-Hill.

This how-to book by a professional counselor and trainer encourages negotiation from the win-win perspective. It also suggests possible ways for applying the method to all aspects of life.

151. Wedge, B. 1971. "A psychiatric model of intercession in intergroup conflict." *Journal of Applied Behavioral Science* 7(6):733-761.

The author proposes a five-step process model for intercession in intergroup conflict. He reports the results of an application of the theory at the international level, between the U.S. Embassy and residents of the Dominican Republic. In addition, he recommends the creation of peace-making as a science.

152. Wickstom, R.A. 1979. "Participation revisited: Who decides, when, and how much." *Canadian Administrator* 19(2):1-4.

This article notes that conflicts arise in a participative decision making process. The author suggests when the need for participation is, or is not, indicated.

153. Witty, C.J. 1980. *Mediation and Society: Conflict management in Lebanon*. New York: Academic Press.

Mediation is a technique of conflict resolution that has not been widely adopted in American communities, though it has been implemented in other cultures. Witty presents a theoretical and empirical inquiry into the nature of mediation and its relationship to communities in a Middle Eastern culture. The materials easily generalize a theory of mediation and should be of interest to researchers and practitioners.

154. Zartman, I.W. 1982. *The Practical Negotiator*. New Haven, Conn.: Yale University Press.

After interviewing experienced negotiators, the author presents a three-stage model of negotiation: 1) pre-negotiating, 2) developing a format, and 3) clarifying details. He suggests strategies for each stage and emphasizes the importance of understanding how cultural variables affect the negotiation.

155. Zirkel, P.A. and Lutz, J.G. 1981. "Characteristics and functions of mediators: A pilot study." *Arbitration Journal* 36(2):15-20.

The authors conducted a survey of Connecticut representatives of boards of education and teacher organizations as well as mediators. Their selection of the mediators was based on the mediators' experience either as chiefs of negotiating teams or as participants in cases presented to the State Department of Education.
The authors ranked 14 characteristics in order of their importance for an effective mediation process. Their findings indicate a need both to refine and expand future studies and to determine and develop a systematic program for ideal training in mediation. Much of the effort now underway to develop a National Peace Academy supports this view.

156. Zwingle, J.L. 1980. "Resolving conflict in the upper echelons." In <u>New Directions for Higher Education no.32 (Resolving conflict in higher education)</u> 8(4):33-42.

The author reviews problems that occur among university board members and between board members and presidents. He suggests third-party intervention and presents examples for application.

CITATIONS

Aaronson, D.E., et al. 1975. The New Justice: Alternatives to conventional criminal adjudication. Washington, D.C.: National Institute of Law Enforcement and Criminal Justice, Law Enforcement Assistance Administration, U.S. Department of Justice.

Abel, R.L. 1973. "A comparative theory of dispute institutions in society." Law and Society Review 8(2):217-347.

Abner, W. 1969. "The FMCS and dispute mediation in the federal government." Monthly Labor Review 92(5):27-29.

Adams, G.W. 1978. "Grievance arbitration of discharge cases: A study of the concepts of industrial discipline and their results." In Research and Current Issues Series no. 38. Kingston, Ontario: Queen's University, Industrial Relations Centre.

Aguilera, D.C. and Messick, J.M. 1982. Crisis Intervention: Theory and methodology, 4th ed. St. Louis, Mo.: C.V. Mosby Co.

Alaska Judicial Council. 1977. Anchorage (Alaska) Citizen Dispute Center: A needs assessment and feasibility report. Anchorage: AJC.

Alberta Conciliation Services. 1975. Demonstration Project, #558-1-12. Ottawa, Canada: National Health and Welfare.

Alper, B.S. and Nichols, L.T. 1981. Beyond the Courtroom: Programs in community justice and conflict resolution. Lexington, Mass.: Lexington Books/D.C. Heath.

American Arbitration Association, Office of the General Counsel. 1982. Arbitration and the Law. New York: AAA.

American Bar Association. 1979. Dispute Resolution Act - Amendment. Washington, D.C.: ABA, Division of Public Service Activities.

Anderson, B.E. 1980. "Challenges to collective bargaining." Labor Law Journal 31(8):470-472.

Anderson, D.B. 1978. "Conflict intervention." In Tools for Trainers: Training tools and lesson plans, 1978. Carbondale: Southern Illinois University Center for the Study of Crime, Delinquency and Corrections.

Anderson, J.C. 1981. "Impact of arbitration: A methodological assessment." Industrial Relations 20(2):129-148.

Angoff, S.E. 1961. "Impartial opinion and constructive criticism of mediators, mediation agencies, and conciliators." Labor Law Journal 12(1):67-72.

Applied Communication, Argumentation, and Debate: Abstracts of Doctoral Dissertations. In Dissertation Abstracts International, vol. 40, nos. 7-12.

40

? Aram, J.D. and Salipante, P.F., Jr. 1981. "An evaluation of organizational due process in the resolution of employee/employer conflict." *Academy of Management Review* 6(2):197-204.

Arendt, H. 1970. *On Violence*. New York: Harcourt, Brace & World.

Australia Information Service. 1978. "Industrial Arbitration." Canberra: Australia Government Publishing Service.

Axelberd, M.M. 1979. "The effects of family crisis intervention training on police behavior and level of anxiety in response to a domestic dispute." *Dissertation Abstracts International* 38(11-B):5536.

Axelrod, R. 1970. *Conflict of Interest: A theory of divergent goals with applications to politics*. Chicago: Markham Publishing Co.

Azrin, N.H. and Besalel, V.A. 1980. "Comparison of reciprocity and discussion-type counseling for marital problems." *The American Journal of Family Therapy* 8(4):21-28.

Bacharach, S.B. and Lawler, E.J. 1980. *Power and Politics in Organizations: The social psychology of conflict, coalitions, and bargaining*. San Francisco: Jossey-Bass.

Bacharach, S.B. and Lawler, E.J. 1981. "Bargaining: Power, tactics, and outcomes." Washington, D.C.: National Science Foundation.

Bacharach, S.B. and Lawler, E.J. 1981. "Power and tactics in bargaining." *Industry and Labor Relations Review* 34(2):219-233.

Bagarozzi, D.A. and Wodarski, J.S. 1978. "Behavioral treatment of marital discord." *Clinical Social Work Journal* 6(2):135-154.

Bard, M. 1980. "Functions of the police and the justice system in family violence." In *Violence and the Family*, edited by M.R. Green. Boulder, Colo.: Westview Press.

Bard, M. and Zacker, J. 1978. "How police handle explosive squabbles." In *Criminal Justice, 1978-1979 - Annual Editions*, edited by E.J. Donald MacNamara. Guilford, Conn.: Duskin Publishing Group, Inc.

? Bateman, T.S. 1980. "Contingent concession strategies in dyadic bargaining." *Organizational Behavior and Human Performance* 26(2):212-221.

Baumgartner, T.; Burns, T.R.; and DeVille, P. 1978. "Conflict resolution and conflict development: A theory of game transformation with an application to the LIP factory conflict." *Research in Social Movements, Conflicts and Change* 1:105-142.

Baxter, L.A. and Shepherd, T.L. 1978. "Sex-role identity, sex of other, and affective relationship as determinants of interpersonal conflict-management styles." *Sex Roles* 4(6):813-825.

Beal, D.; Gillis, J.S.; and Stewart, T. 1978. "The lens model: Computational procedures and applications." *Perceptual and Motor Skills* 46(1):3-28.

Beauchamp, T.L. and Bowie, N.E., eds. 1979. *Ethical Theory and Business*. Englewood Cliffs, N.J.: Prentice-Hall.

Begin, J.P. 1980. "The development of the neutral function in labor relations." *New Directions for Higher Education*, no. 32 (Resolving Conflict in Higher Education) 8(4):81-89.

Behavioral Research Associates. 1978. *Visionquest: Program Description, 1978*. Tucson, Ariz.: BRA.

Benjamin, A.J. and Levi, A.M. 1979. "Process minefields in intergroup conflict resolution: The Sdot Yam workshop." *Journal of Applied Behavioral Science* 15(4):507-519.

Bennett, G.C. 1979. "The heckler and the heckled in the presidential campaign of 1968." *Communication Quarterly* 27(2):28-37.

Beresford, R. and Cooper, J. 1977. "A neighborhood court for neighborhood suits." *Judicature* 61(4):185-190.

Berger, P.L. and Neuhaus, R.J. 1977. *To Empower People: The role of mediating structures in public policy*. Washington, D.C.: American Enterprise Institute for Public Policy Research.

Bergman, R.D. 1978. *Social Conflict and Mental Health Services*. Springfield, Ill.: Charles C. Thomas, Publishers.

Berlew, D.E. and LeClere, W.E. 1974. "Social intervention in Curacao: A case study." *Journal of Applied Behavioral Science* 10(1):29-52.

Berlin, R.J. 1978. "Teaching acting-out adolescents prosocial conflict resolution through structured learning training of empathy." *Dissertation Abstracts International* 39(2-B):970.

Bermant, G.; Kelman, H.C.; and Warwick, D.P. 1978. *The Ethics of Social Intervention*. Washington, D.C.: Hemisphere Publishing Corp.

Bernard, J. 1954. "The theory of games of strategy as a modern sociology of conflict." *American Journal of Sociology* 59(5):411-424.

Bernard, J. 1965. "Some current conceptualizations in the field of conflict." *American Journal of Sociology* 70(4):442-454.

Billings, A. 1979. "Conflict resolution in distressed and nondistressed married couples." *Journal of Consulting and Clinical Psychology* 47(2):368-376.

Bion, W.R. 1961. *Experiences in Groups, and Other Papers*. New York: Basic Books.

Birnbaum, R. 1980. "Constructive conflict in academic bargaining." In *New Directions for Higher Education*, no. 32 (Resolving Conflict in Higher Education) 8(4):69-79.

Birnbaum, R. 1980. <u>Creative Academic Bargaining: Managing conflict in the unionized college and university</u>. New York: Columbia University, Teachers College Press.

Blake, R.R. and Mouton, J.S. 1962. "The intergroup dynamics of win-lose conflict and problem-solving collaboration in union-management relations." In <u>Intergroup Relations and Leadership: Approaches and research in industrial, ethnic, cultural, and political areas</u>, edited by M. Sherif. New York: John Wiley & Sons.

Blake, R.R. and Mouton, J.S. 1970. "The fifth achievement." <u>Journal of Applied Behavioral Science</u> 6(4):413-426.

Blake, R.R.; Mouton, J.S.; and Sloma, R.L. 1965. "The union-management intergroup laboratory: Strategy for resolving intergroup conflict." <u>Journal of Applied Behavioral Science</u> 1(1):25-57.

Blake, R.R.; Shepard, H.A.; and Mouton, J.S. 1964. <u>Managing Intergroup Conflict in Industry</u>. Houston, Tex.: Gulf Publishing Co.

Blanchard, R. 1981. "Settling international contract dispute through arbitration." <u>International Management</u> 36(5):45-46.

Blechman, E.A. 1980. "Family problem-solving training." <u>The American Journal of Family Therapy</u> 8(3):3-21.

Blomberg, T.G. 1977. "Diversion and accelerated social control." <u>Journal of Criminal Law and Criminology</u> 68(2):274-282.

Blomberg, T.G. and Caraballo, S.L. 1979. "Accelerated family intervention in juvenile justice: An exploration and a recommendation for constraint." <u>Crime and Delinquency</u> 25(4):497-502.

Blood, R.O., Jr. 1960. "Resolving family conflicts." <u>Journal of Conflict Resolution</u> 4(2):209-219.

* Bloom, D.E. 1981. "Is arbitration <u>really</u> compatible with bargaining?" <u>Industrial Relations</u> 20(3):233-244.

Bloom, M. 1978. "Conciliation court: Crisis intervention in domestic violence." <u>Crime Prevention Review</u> 6(1):19-27.

Blumrosen, A.W. 1972. "Civil rights conflicts: The uneasy search for peace in our time." <u>The Arbitration Journal</u> 27(1):35-46.

Bok, S. 1978. <u>Lying: Moral choice in public and private life</u>. New York: Pantheon Books.

Bonoma, T.V. and Milburn, T.W. 1977. "Social conflict: Another look." <u>Journal of Social Issues</u> 33(1):1-8.

* Boulding, E., ed. 1961. <u>Conflict Management in Organizations</u>. New York: Basic Books.

Boulding, K.E. 1957. "Organization and conflict." <u>Journal of Conflict Resolution</u> 1(2):122-134.

Boulding, K.E. 1962. Conflict and Defense: A general theory. New York: Harper & Row.

Boulding, K.E. 1964. "Two principles of conflict." In Power and Conflict in Organizations, edited by R.L. Kahn and E. Boulding. New York: Basic Books.

Boulding, K.E. 1965. "The economics of human conflict." In The Nature of Human Conflict, edited by Elton B. McNeil. Englewood Cliffs, N.J.: Prentice-Hall.

Boules, A., et al., eds. 1981. Crossroads...A handbook for effective classroom management. Oklahoma City: Oklahoma Department of Education.

Bowen, D.D. 1977. "Value dilemmas in organization development." Journal of Applied Behavioral Science 13(4):543-556.

Boyd, W.L. 1979. "Educational policy making in declining suburban school districts: Some preliminary findings." Education and Urban Society 11(3):333-366.

Braun, C.T., et al. 1981. "Communication conflict predisposition: Development of a theory and an instrument." Human Relations 34(12):1103-1117.

Braver, S.L. and Rohrer, V. 1978. "Superiority of vicarious over direct experience in interpersonal conflict resolution." Journal of Conflict Resolution 22(1):143-155.

Breaugh, J.A. 1980. "Third party characteristics and intergroup conflict resolution." Psychological Reports 47(2)447-451.

Brickman, P., ed. 1974. Social Conflict: Readings in role structures and conflict relationships. Lexington, Mass.: Lexington Books/D.C. Heath.

Bridenback, M.L.; Palmer, K.R.; and Planchard, J.B. 1979. "Citizen dispute settlement: The Florida experience." American Bar Association Journal 65(4):570-573.

Briggs, W.A. 1979. "School racial and ethnic conflict prevention." Crime Prevention Review 6(3):21-25.

Broderick, C.B., ed. 1971. A Decade of Family Research and Action, 1960-1969. Minneapolis: National Council on Family Relations.

Brookmire, D.A. and Sistrunk, F. 1980. "The effects of perceived ability and impartiality of mediators and time pressure on negotiation." Journal of Conflict Resolution 24(2):311-327.

Brooks, D.; Winsor, J.; and Shoemaker, T. 1980. "Interpersonal communication and human relations training for corrections personnel." Communication Education 29(1):54-60.

Brown, E.C. 1979. "Evaluation of the Akron 4-A project." In Resolution of Major Disputes. Washington, D.C.: U.S. Congress House Subcommittee on Courts, Civil Liberties, and the Administration of Justice.

Brown, L.D. 1980. "Planned change in underorganized systems." In *Systems Theory for Organization Development*, edited by T.G. Cummings. New York: John Wiley & Sons.

Brown, L.D.; Aram, J.D.; and Bachner, D.J. 1974. "Interorganizational information sharing: A successful intervention that failed." *Journal of Applied Behavioral Science* 10(4):533-554.

Bucholz, E. 1980. "The social courts in the German Democratic Republic: Bodies of criminal justice." *International Journal of Comparative and Applied Criminal Justice* 4(1):37-42.

Burns, T.R. and Buckley, W., eds. 1976. *Power and Control: Social structures and their transformation*. Beverly Hills, Calif.: Sage Publications.

Butler, A.S. 1980. "A conflict management training program for school psychologists." *Dissertation Abstracts International* 40(11-B):5388.

Byng-Hall, J. and Campbell, D. 1981. "Resolving conflicts in family distance regulation: An interpretive approach." *Journal of Marital and Family Therapy* 7(3):321-330.

California Department of the Youth Authority. 1978. *Gang Violence Reduction Project: First evaluation report, November 1976 - September 1977*. Washington, D.C.: U.S. Department of Justice, Law Enforcement Assistance Administration.

Cannizzo, C. 1979. "Quantitative international conflict studies: A look at the record." *Armed Forces and Society* 6(1):111-121.

Cantor, I. and Ferguson, P.L. 1976. "From the judge's view--Family counseling in the conciliation court: An alternative to custody litigation." *Conciliation Courts Review* 14(1):1-16.

Center for Women Policy Studies. 1978. *Spouse Abuse in the Legal System: Selected readings*. Rockville, Md.: National Criminal Justice Reference Service, Microfiche Program, Box 6000.

Chafetz, J.S. 1980. "Conflict resolution in marriage: Toward a theory of spousal strategies and marital dissolution rates." *Journal of Family Issues* 1(3):397-421.

Chalmers, W.E. 1974. *Racial Negotiations: Potentials and limitations*. Ann Arbor: Institute of Labor and Industrial Relations, The University of Michigan-Wayne State.

Chalmers, W.E. and Cormick, G.W. 1971. *Racial Conflict and Negotiations: Perspectives and first-case studies*. Ann Arbor: Institute of Labor and Industrial Relations, The University of Michigan-Wayne State University.

Chatterjee, K. 1981. "Comparison of arbitration procedures: Models with complete and incomplete information." *IEEE Transactions on Systems, Man, and Cybernetics* 11(2):101-109.

Chelius, J.R. and Dworkin, J.B. 1980. "An economic analysis of final-offer arbitration as a conflict resolution device." *Journal of Conflict Resolution* 24(2):293-310.

Chesler, M.A.; Crowfoot, J.E.; and Bryant, B.I. 1978. "Power training: An alternative path to conflict management." *California Management Review* 21(2):84-90.

Chesney, S.L. 1976. *Assessment of Restitution in the Minnesota Probation Services: Summary report*. St. Paul: Minnesota Department of Corrections.

Church, T.W., Jr.; Carleson, A.; Lee, J.L.; and Tan, T. 1978. *Justice Delayed: The pace of litigation in urban trial courts*. Williamsburg, Va.: National Center for State Courts.

Cisek, J.V. 1979. "The effects of teaching conflict management and interpersonal problem solving skills to junior high school students." *Dissertation Abstracts International* 39(12-A):7159.

Clegg, S. 1979. *The Theory of Power and Organization*. London: Routledge and Kegan Paul.

Clemons, A.H. 1980. "A validity and reliability study of the conflict management survey in educational settings." *Dissertation Abstracts International* 41(11-A):864.

Clower, J. and Goodwin, G.C. 1982. "A theory of organizational behavior applied to college housing." *College Student Journal* 16(1):73-76.

Cohen, H. 1980. *You Can Negotiate Anything*. Secaucus, N.J.: Lyle Stuart.

Cole, D.L. 1963. *The Quest for Industrial Peace*. New York: McGraw-Hill Co.

Coleman, J.S. 1957. *Community Conflict*. New York: The Free Press.

Collett, C.S. 1979. "A comparison of the effects of marital and family enrichment programs on self-concept and conflict resolution ability." *Dissertation Abstracts International* 40(6-A):3113.

Collins, B.E. and Guetzkow, H. 1964. *A Social Psychology of Group Processes for Decision-Making*. New York: John Wiley & Sons.

Collons, R.D. 1982. "Mediation and problem solving." *Best's Review Life/Health Insurance Edition* 82(10):106-108.

Colson, C.W. and Benson, D.H. 1980. "Restitution as an alternative to imprisonment." *Detroit College Law Review* 2:523-598.

Conn, S. and Hippler, A.E. 1974. "Conciliation and arbitration in the native village and the urban ghetto." *Judicature* 58(5):228-235.

Conner, R.F. and Surette, R. 1977. *Alternatives to Court: An evaluation of the Orange County (Florida) Bar Association's citizen dispute settlement program*. Washington, D.C.: American Bar Association.

Coogler, O.J. 1978. <u>Structured Mediation in Divorce Settlement: A handbook for divorce mediators</u>. Lexington, Mass: Lexington Books/D.C. Heath.

Cook, D.D. 1976. "Is federal mediation hurting labor-management relations?" <u>Industry Week</u> 190(6):17-23.

Coons, J.E. 1980. "Compromise as precise justice." <u>California Law Review</u> 68(2):250-262.

Corsini, R.J. 1978. "Impossible cases." <u>Individual Psychologists</u> 15(1):5-10.

Coser, L.A. 1956. <u>The Functions of Social Conflict</u>. New York: The Free Press.

Coser, L.A. 1961. "The termination of conflict." <u>Journal of Conflict Resolution</u> 5(4):347-353.

Coser, L.A. 1967. <u>Continuities in the Study of Social Conflict</u>. New York: The Free Press.

Cosier, R.A. and Ruble, T.L. 1981. "Research on conflict handling behavior: An experimental approach." <u>Academy of Management Journal</u> 24(4):816-831.

Cotchett, J.W. 1978. "Community courts: A viable concept." <u>Trial</u> 14(4):45-57.

Coulson, R. 1968. <u>How to Stay Out of Court</u>. New York: Crown Publishers.

Coulson, R. 1980. "New views of arbitration: Satisfying the demands of the employee." <u>Labor Law Journal</u> 31(8):495-497.

Courtright, J.A. 1978. "A laboratory investigation of groupthink." <u>Communication Monographs</u> 45(3):229-246.

Cox, H. and Wood, J.R. 1980. "Organizational structure and professional alienation: The case of public school teachers." <u>Peabody Journal of Education</u> 58(1):1-6.

Cratsley, J.C. 1978. "Community courts: Offering alternative dispute resolution within the judicial system." <u>Vermont Law Review</u> 3(1):1-69.

Crawford, V.P. 1981. "Arbitration and conflict resolution in labor-management bargaining." <u>American Economic Review</u> 71(2):205-210.

Crockenberg, S.B. and Nicolayev, J. 1970. "Stage transition in moral reasoning as related to conflict experienced in naturalistic settings." <u>Merrill-Palmer Quarterly</u> 25(3):185-192.

Cromwell, R.E. and Olson, D.H., eds. 1975. <u>Power in Families</u>. New York: John Wiley & Sons.

Cromwell, V.L. and Cromwell, R.E. 1978. "Perceived dominance in decision-making and conflict resolution among Anglo, Black and Chicano couples." <u>Journal of Marriage and the Family</u> 40(4):749-759.

Cullinane, M.J. 1978. "Terrorism: A new area of criminality." *Terrorism* 1(2):119-124.

Cummings, L.L.; Harnett, D.L.; and Stevens, O.J. 1971. "Risk, fate, conciliation, and trust: An international study of attitudinal differences among executives." *Academy of Management Journal* 14(3):285-304.

Daley, J.M. and Keltner, P.M. 1981. "Bargaining in community development." *Journal of the Community Development Society* 12(2):25-38.

Danzig, R. and Lowy, M.J. 1975. "Everyday disputes and mediation in the United States: A reply to Professor Felstiner." *Law and Society Review* 9(4):675-694.

Davies, J.C. 1962. "Toward a theory of revolution." *American Sociological Review* 27(1):5-19.

DeCecco, J.P. and Roberts, J. 1978. "Negotiating school conflict to prevent student delinquency." In *School Crime and Disruption*, edited by E. Wenk and N. Harlow. Davis, Calif.: Responsible Action.

DeCecco, J.P. and Schaeffer, G.A. 1978. "Using negotiation to resolve teacher-student conflicts." *Journal of Research and Development in Education* 11(4):64-77.

DeCecco, J. and Shively, M.G. 1978. "A study of perceptions of rights and needs in interpersonal conflicts in homosexual relationships." *Journal of Homosexuality* 3(3):205-215.

Dedring, J. 1976. *Recent Advances in Peace and Conflict Research: A Critical Survey*. Beverly Hills, Calif.: Sage Publications.

DeNisi, A.S. and Dworkin, J.B. 1981. "Final-offer arbitration and the naive negotiator." *Industry and Labor Relations Review* 35(1):78-87.

Derdeyn, A.P. and Waters, D.B. 1981. "Unshared loss and marital conflict." *Journal of Marital and Family Therapy* 7(4):481-487.

Derr, C.B. 1978. "Managing organizational conflict: Collaboration, bargaining, and power approaches." *California Management Review* 21(2):76-83.

de Reuck, A. and Knight, J., eds. 1966. *Conflict in Society: A Ciba Foundation volume*. London: J&A Churchill.

Deutsch, M. 1969. "Conflicts: Productive and destructive." *Journal of Social Issues* 25(1):7-41.

Deutsch, M. 1973. *The Resolution of Conflict: Constructive and destructive processes*. New Haven, Conn.: Yale University Press.

Dewar, R. and Werbel, J. 1979. "Universalistic and contingency predictions of employee satisfaction and conflict." *Administrative Science Quarterly* 24(3):426-448.

Diesing, P. 1961. "Bargaining strategy and union-management relationships." Journal of Conflict Resolution 5(4):369-378.

Dodson, D.W. 1958. "The creative role of conflict in intergroup relations." The Merrill-Palmer Quarterly 4(4):189-195.

Dodson, D.W. 1959. "The creative role of conflict reexamined." The Journal of Intergroup Relations 1(1):5-12.

Doering, W.R. 1980. "Levels of conflict among health care personnel." Dissertation Abstracts International 40(9-B):4195.

Doherty, W.J. 1981. "Cognitive processes in intimate conflict: II, Efficiency and learned helplessness." The Journal of Family Therapy 9(2):35-43.

Donaldson, T. and Werthane, P.H. 1979. Ethical Issues in Business: A philosophical approach. Englewood Cliffs, N.J.: Prentice-Hall.

Doo, L.W. 1973. "Dispute settlement in Chinese-American communities." American Journal of Comparative Law 21:627-663.

Doremus, D.B. 1978. "The relationship between elementary principal role conflict and ambiguity and organizational behavior." Dissertation Abstracts International 38(12-A):7046-7047.

Dorr, J.V.N. 1981. "Labor arbitrator training: The internship." Arbitration Journal 36(2):4-10.

* Douglas, A. 1962. Industrial Peacemaking. New York: Columbia University Press.

Doyle, B. 1980. "A substitute for collective bargaining? The central arbitration committee's approach to section 16 of the Employment Protection Act 1975." Industrial Law Journal 9:154-166.

Doyle, M. and Straus, D. 1976. How to Make Meetings Work: The new interaction method. New York: Wyden Books.

Driscoll, J.M.; Meyer, R.G.; and Schanie, C.F. 1973. "Training police in family crisis intervention." Journal of Applied Behavioral Science 9(1):62-82.

* Druckman, D. 1967. "Dogmatism, prenegotiation experience, and simulated group representation as determinants of dyadic behavior in a bargaining situation." Journal of Personality and Social Psychology 6(3):279-290.

Druckman, D., ed. 1977. Negotiations: Social-psychological perspectives. Beverly Hills, Calif.: Sage Publications.

Dubois, P.L., ed. 1982. The Analysis of Judicial Reform. Lexington, Mass.: Lexington Books/D.C. Heath.

Duffy, F.M., Jr. 1980. "An analysis of conflict and conflict resolution in relation to effectiveness and efficiency in diagnostic conferences between supervisors and teachers." Dissertation Abstracts International 40(8-A):4323.

Duke, J.T. 1976. Conflict and Power in Social Life. Provo, Utah: Brigham Young University Press.

Ebel, D.M. 1979. "Landlord-tenant mediation project in Colorado." Urban Law Annual 17:279-286.

Eckhoff, T. 1967. "The mediator, the judge, and the administrator in conflict-resolution." Acta Sociologica 10(3):148-172.

Edmonton Family Court Conciliation Service. 1978. The Edmonton (Canada) Family Court Marriage Conciliation Service: Five-year summary of operations, 1972-1977. Edmonton, Alberta: EFCCS.

Edwards, R. 1979. Contested Terrain: The transformation of the workplace in the Twentieth Century. New York: Basic Books.

Eekelaar, J.M. and Katz, S.N., eds. 1978. Family Violence: An international and interdisciplinary study. Toronto: Butterworths.

Eiseman, J.W. 1977. "A third-party consultation model for resolving recurring conflicts collaboratively." Journal of Applied Behavioral Science 13(3):303-314.

Eiseman, J.W. 1978. "Reconciling 'incompatible' positions." Journal of Applied Behavioral Science 14(2):133-150.

Elder, G.J., Jr. 1963. "Parental power legitimation and its effect on the adolescent." Sociometry 26(1):50-65.

Eldridge, A.F. 1979. Images of Conflict. New York: St. Martin's Press.

Fagin, J.A. 1978. "The effects of police interpersonal communication skills on conflict resolution." Dissertation Abstracts International 39(4-A):1924.

Fahey, R.P. 1975. "Native American justice: The courts of the Navajo Nation." Judicature 59(1):10-17.

Farber, H.S. 1981. "Role of arbitration in dispute settlement." Monthly Labor Review 104(5):34-36.

Faucheux, C. and Rojot, J. 1979. "Social psychology and industrial relations: A cross-cultural perspective." Industrial Relations: A social psychological approach. New York: John Wiley & Sons.

Feinsinger, N.P. 1956. "Private mediation: Its potential." Labor Law Journal 7(8):493-496.

Felstiner, W. 1974. "Influences of social organization on dispute processing." Law and Society Review 9(1):63-94.

Felstiner, W. 1975. "Avoidance as dispute processing: An elaboration." Law and Society Review 9(3):695-706.

Feltner, B.D. and Goodsell, D.R. 1972. "The academic dean and conflict management." *Journal of Higher Education* 43(9):692-701.

Ferguson, C.K. 1968. "Concerning the nature of human systems and the consultant's role." *Journal of Applied Behavioral Science* 4(2):179-193.

Feuille, P. 1977. "Final-offer arbitration and negotiating incentives." *Arbitration Journal* 32(3):203-220.

Filley, A.C. 1975. *Interpersonal Conflict Resolution*. Glenview, Ill.: Scott, Foresman and Co.

Filley, A.C. 1977. "Conflict resolution: The ethic of the good loser." In *Readings in Interpersonal and Organizational Communication*, edited by R.C. Huseman, C.M. Logue, and D.L. Freshly. Boston, Mass.: Holbrook Press.

Filley, A.C. 1978. "Some normative issues in conflict management." *California Management Review* 21(2):61-66.

Fink, C.F. 1968. "Some conceptual difficulties in the theory of social conflict." *Journal of Conflict Resolution* 12(4):412-460.

Fink, S.L.; Beak, J.; and Taddeo, K. 1971. "Organizational crisis and change." *Journal of Applied Behavioral Science* 7(1):15-37.

Fiorito, B.A. 1978. "Marital interaction among high and low adjusted couples: A comparison of participants and observer perceptions." *Dissertation Abstracts International* 39(2-A):1135.

Fisher, E.A. 1975. "Community courts: An alternative to conventional criminal adjudication." *American University Law Review* 24(4-5):1253-1291.

Fisher, R.J. 1972. "Third-party consultation: A method for the study and resolution of conflict." *Journal of Conflict Resolution* 16(1):67-94.

Fisher, R. 1981. *Getting to Yes: Negotiating agreement without giving in*. Boston, Mass.: Houghton, Mifflin Co.

Fitzpatrick, M.A. and Winke, J. 1979. "You always hurt the one you love: Strategies and tactics in interpersonal conflict." *Communication Quarterly* 27(1):3-11.

Fleishman, J.L.; Liebman, L.; and Moore, M.H., eds. 1981. *Public Duties: The moral obligations of government officials*. Cambridge, Mass.: Harvard University Press.

Florida Office of the State Courts Administrator. 1979. *Citizen Dispute Settlement Process in Florida: A study of five programs*. Tallahassee: FOSCA.

Follett, M.P. 1942. "Constructive conflict." In *Dynamic Administration: The collected papers of Mary Parker Follett*, edited by H.C. Metcalf and L. Urwick. New York: Harper & Row.

Forbes, F.S. 1980. "Arbitration of small business disputes: The potential for Nebraska." *Arbitration Journal* 35(1):17-24.

Ford Foundation. 1978. *Mediating Social Conflict: A Ford Foundation report*. New York: Ford Foundation Press.

Ford Foundation. 1978. *New Approaches to Conflict Resolution*. New York: Ford Foundation Press.

Ford Foundation. 1979. *Access to Justice, vol. 4. Anthropological Perspective Patterns of Conflict Management: Essays in the ethnography of law*. Alphen Aan Den Rijn, Netherlands: Sijthoff and Noordhoff.

Foster, S.L. 1979. "Family conflict management: Skill training and generalization procedures." *Dissertation Abstracts International* 39(10-B):5063-5064.

Frankel, M.E. 1976. "From private fights toward public justice." *New York University Law Review* 51(4):516-537.

Freedman, S.C. 1981. "Threats, promises, and coalitions: A study of compliance and retaliation in a simulated organizational setting." *Journal of Applied Social Psychology* 11(2):114-136.

Frey, J.; Holley, J.; and L'Abate, L. 1979. "Intimacy is sharing hurt feelings: A comparison of three conflict resolution models." *Journal of Marital and Family Therapy* 5(2):35-41.

Frey, R.L., Jr., and Adams, J.S. 1972. "The negotiator's dilemma: Simultaneous in-group and out-group conflict." *Journal of Experimental Social Psychology* 8(4):331-346.

Friedman, A. 1977. "The effectiveness of arbitration for the resolution of consumer disputes." *New York University Review of Law and Social Change* 6(2):175-215.

Friedman, M. 1979. "Problems of cross-examination in labor arbitration." *Arbitration Journal* 34(4):6-11.

Frost, J.H. 1981. *Interpersonal Conflict*. Dubuque, Iowa: W.C. Brown Co.

Fry, L.W.; Kirdon, A.G.; Osborn, R.N.; and Trafton, R.S. 1980. "A constructive replication of the Lawrence and Lorsch conflict resolution methodology." *Journal of Management* 6(1):7-19.

Fuller, L.L. 1971. "Mediation: Its forms and functions." *Southern California Law Review* 44(2):305-339. *good overview of med. from legal standpoint*

Fuller, L.L. 1978. "The forms and limits of adjudication." *Harvard Law Review* 92(2):353-409.

Galanter, M. 1974. "Why the 'have's' come out ahead: Speculations on the limits of legal change." *Law and Society Review* 9(1):95-160.

Galanter, M. 1975. "Afterword: Explaining litigation." *Law and Society Review* 9(2):347-368.

Galassi, J.P.; Galassi, M.D.; and Westfeld, J.S. 1978. "The Conflict Resolution Inventory: Psychometric data." *Psychological Reports* 42(2):492-494.

Galin, A. and Krislov, J. 1979. "Evaluating the Israeli mediation service." *International Labour Review* 118(4):487-497.

Galin, A. and Krislov, J. 1979. "Mediation techniques in four countries." *Labor Studies Journal* 4:119-130.

Gallagher, D.G. and Chaubey, M.D. 1982. "Impasse behavior and tri-offer arbitration in Iowa." *Industrial Relations* 21(2):129-148.

Gamson, W.A. 1961. "An experimental test of a theory of coalition formation." *American Sociological Review* 26(4):565-573.

Gamson, W.A. 1964. "Experimental studies of coalition formation." *Advances in Experimental Social Psychology* 1:81-110.

Gamson, W.A. 1966. "Rancorous conflict in community politics." *American Sociological Review* 31(1):71-81.

Gamson, W.A. 1975. *The Strategy of Social Protest*. Homewood, Ill.: Dorsey Press.

Garofalo, J. and Connelly, K.J. 1980. "Dispute resolution centers, part 1: Major features and processes." *Criminal Justice Abstracts* 12(3):416-439.

Gaudreau, G.C. 1976. "The effectiveness of mediation and arbitration of teacher-school board disagreements in Connecticut as perceived by the parties involved." *Dissertation Abstracts International* 37(2-A):730-731.

Geare, A.J. 1978. "Final offer arbitration: A critical examination of the theory." *Journal of Industrial Relations* 20(4):373-385.

Gerhart, P.F. and Drotning, J.E. 1980. "Dispute settlement and the intensity of mediation." *Industrial Relations* 19(3):352-359.

Gettone, V.G. 1978. "Conflict resolutions among student teachers: Dogmatism as a related factor." *Dissertation Abstracts International* 38(7-A):4043-4044.

Gilroy, T.P. and Sinicropi, A.V. 1972. *Dispute Settlement in the Public Sector: The state of the art*. Washington, D.C.: Government Printing Office.

Gilroy, T.P. and Sinicropi, A.V., eds. 1970. *Collective Negotiations and Public Administration*. Conference Series No. 15. Iowa City: Center for Labor and Management, University of Iowa.

Gitelson, P. 1979. "Model program to avoid institutionalization of children." *Journal of Sociology and Social Welfare* 6(6):805-813.

Glickman, C.D. and Wolfgang, C.H. 1978. "Conflict in the classroom: An eclectic model of teacher-child interaction." *Elementary School Guidance Counseling* 13(2):82-87.

Glynn, M.M. 1978. "Arbitration of landlord-tenant disputes." American University Law Review 27(2):407-432.

Gold, L. 1981. "Mediation in the dissolution of marriage." Arbitration Journal 36(3):9-13.

Goldaber, I. 1980. "Community involvement in school closings: A new approach to a growing problem." Updating School Board Policies 11(8):1-3,5.

Goldbeck, W.B. 1975. "Mediation: An instrument of citizen involvement." Arbitration Journal 30(4):241-252.

Goldman, H.H. 1978. "Within and between: The role of the psychiatric resident in the psychiatric unit in the general hospital: A case study of systemic conflict and its management." Dissertation Abstracts International 39(5-B):2222.

Goldman, S. and Sarat, A., eds. 1978. American Court Systems: Readings in judicial process and behavior. San Francisco: W.H. Freeman.

Goldmann, R.B., ed. 1980. Roundtable Justice: Case studies in conflict resolution. Boulder, Colo.: Westview Press.

Goldstein, N. 1974. "Reparation by the offender to the victim as a method of rehabilitation for both." In Victimology: A new focus, vol. 2, edited by I. Drapkin and E. Viano. Lexington, Mass.: Lexington Books/D.C. Heath.

Golembiewski, R.T. 1978. "Managing the tension between OD principles and political dynamics." In The Cutting Edge: Current theory and practice in organizational development, edited by W.W. Burke. La Jolla, Calif.: University Associates.

Golembiewski, R.T. 1979. Approaches to Planned Change. (Two volumes: Part 1: Orienting perspectives and micro-level interventions. Part 2: Macro-level interventions and change-agent strategies.) New York: Marcel Dekker.

Golembiewski, R.T.; Tattner, J.B.; and Miller, G.J. 1979. "Designing an arbitration system for a mass transportation construction project." Arbitration Journal 34(3):14-24.

Goodge, P. 1978. "Intergroup conflict: A rethink." Human Relations 31(6):475-487.

Gould, W.B. 1969. "Public employment: Mediation, fact-finding, and arbitration." American Bar Association Journal 55(9):835-841.

Grace, W.V.N., Jr. 1980. "The effects of an interactive computer simulator (KSIM) upon the resolution of mixed conflict in a negotiation situation." Dissertation Abstracts International 40(10-A):5247.

Graham, H. and Wallace, V. 1982. "Trends in public sector arbitration." Personnel Administrator 27(4):73-77.

Green, M.R., ed. 1980. Violence and the Family. Boulder, Colo.: Westview Press.

Greenberg, L.S. and Higgins, H.M. 1980. "Effects of two-chair dialogue and focusing on conflict resolution." Journal of Counseling Psychology 27(3):221-224.

Gricar, B.G. and Brown, D.L. 1981. "Conflict, power, and organization in a changing community." Human Relations 34(10):877-893.

Griffin, G.R.; Rausch, E.; and Wohlking, W. 1978. Handling Conflict in Law Enforcement Management Series. Cranford, N.J.: Didactic Systems.

Gullett, C.R. and Goff, W.H. 1980. "The arbitral decision-making process: A computerized simulation." Personnel Journal 59(8):663-667.

Gulliver, P.H. 1973. "Negotiations as a mode of dispute settlement: Towards a general model." Law and Society Review 7(4):667-691.

Gulliver, P.H. 1979. Disputes and Negotiations: A cross-cultural perspective. New York: Academic Press.

Gustafson, J.P. and Cooper, L. 1981. "Cooperative and clashing interests in small groups." Human Relations 34(4):315-339.

Haizlip, T.M.; Corder, B.F.; and Planavsky, G. 1979. "Hospital-court collaboration in resolving differences over discharges of adolescents." Hospital and Community Psychiatry 30(1):9-13.

Hanami, T.A. 1980. "The settlement of labour disputes in worldwide perspective." International Social Science Journal 32(3):490-504.

Harary, F. and Batell, M.F. 1981. "Communication conflict," Human Relations 34(8):633-641.

Harnett, D.L. and Cummings, L.L. 1980. Bargaining Behavior: An international study. Houston, Tex.: Dame Publications.

Hart, L.B. 1981. Learning from Conflict: A handbook for trainers and group leaders. Reading, Mass.: Addison-Wesley.

Hartnett, T.K.; Mills, M.K.; Newman, H.R.; and Straus, D.B. 1983. "Negotiating by computer." The Arbitration Journal 38(2):3-16.

Hartwig, W.H. 1980. "The assessment of assertiveness: The performance of assertive responses under two discomfort conditions." Dissertation Abstracts International 40(10-B):5003-5004.

Harvey, J.B. 1974. "The Abilene paradox: The management of agreement." Organizational Dynamics 3(1):63-80.

Haw, M.A. 1980. "Conflict resolution and the communication myth." Nursing Outlook 28(9):566-570.

Hay, D.F. and Ross, H.S. 1982. "The social nature of early conflict." Child Development 53(1):105-113.

Hayes, J.L. 1982. "Managing conflict in the organization." Credit and Financial Management 84(2):31-32.

Hayford, S.L. and Pegnetter, R. 1980. "Grievance adjudication for public employees: A comparison of rights arbitration and civil service appeals procedures." Arbitration Journal 35(3):22-29.

Haynes, J.M. 1978. "Divorce mediator: A new role." Social Work 23(1):5-9.

Haynes, J.M. 1981. Divorce Mediation: A practical guide for therapists and counselors. New York: Springer Publishing Co.

Heckathorn, D. 1980. "Unified model for bargaining and conflict." Behavioral Science 25(4):261-284.

Heher, R.J. 1978. "Compulsory judicial arbitration in California: Reducing the delay and expense of resolving uncomplicated civil disputes." Hastings Law Journal 29(3):475-518.

Heintz, D.H. 1979. "Medical malpractice arbitration: A successful hospital-based application." Insurance Law Journal 680:515-523.

Helsilick, R.E. 1979. "Productive conflict in organizations: Cross-cutting memberships and good will." The Wisemun Sociologist 16(4):137-147.

Hepburn, J.R. and Laue, J.H. 1980. "The resolution of inmate grievances as an alternative to the courts." Arbitration Journal 35(1):11-16.

Heppner, P.P. 1978. "A review of the problem-solving literature and its relationship to the counseling process." Journal of Counseling Psychology 25(5):366-375.

Herrman, M.S.; McKenry, P.C.; and Weber, R.E. 1979. "Attorneys' perceptions of their role in divorce." Journal of Divorce 2(3):313-322.

Herrman, M.S.; McKenry, P.C.; and Weber, R.E. 1979. "Mediation and arbitration applied to family conflict resolution: The divorce settlement." The Arbitration Journal 34(1):17-21.

Hermann, C.F., ed. 1972. International Crisis: Insights from Behavioral Research. New York: The Free Press.

Hersey, P. and Blanchard, K.H. 1977. Management of Organizational Behavior: Utilizing human resources, 3d ed. Englewood Cliffs, N.J.: Prentice-Hall.

Hessler, R.M.; New, P.K.; and May, J.T. 1980. "Conflict, consensus and exchange." Social Problems 27(3):320-329.

Himes, J.S. 1966. "The functions of racial conflict." Social Forces 45(1):1-10.

Himes, J.S. 1980. Conflict and Conflict Management. Athens: The University of Georgia Press.

Hirschman, A.O. 1970. Exit, Voice, and Loyalty: Responses to decline in firms, organizations, and states. Cambridge, Mass.: Harvard University Press.

Hocker-Wilmot, J. and Wilmot, W.W. 1978. *Interpersonal Conflict.* Dubuque, Iowa: William C. Brown Co.

Hoellering, M.F. 1982. "The mini-trial." *The Arbitration Journal* 37(4):35-44.

Hofrichter, R. 1980. "Neighborhood justice and the elderly: Policy issues." Washington, D.C.: National Council of Senior Citizens, Criminal Justice and the Elderly Program; U.S. Department of Justice, Law Enforcement Assistance Administration.

Hoh, A.K. 1981. "Consensus-building: A creative approach to resolving conflicts." *Management Review* 70:52-54.

Holland, K. 1982. "The twilight of adversariness: Trends in civil justice." In *The Analysis of Judicial Reform*, edited by P.L. Dubois. Lexington, Mass.: Lexington Books/D.C. Heath.

Horowitz, I.L. 1962. "Consensus, conflict and cooperation: A sociological inventory." *Social Forces* 41(2):177-188.

Horowitz, M. 1964. "Managing hostility in the laboratory and the refinery." In *Power and Conflict in Organizations*, edited by Robert L. Kahn and Elise Boulding. New York: Basic Books.

Houlden, P.; LaTour, S.; Walker, L.; and Thibaut, J. 1978. "Preference for modes of dispute resolution as a function of process and decision control." *Journal of Experimental Social Psychology* 14(1):13-30.

Howat, G.A. 1978. "The relationship between commitment and supervisor-subordinate conflict resolution behavior in Illinois parks and recreation agencies." *Dissertation Abstracts International* 38(10-A):6348-6349.

Howat, G.A. and London, M. 1980. "Attributions of conflict management strategies in supervisor-subordinate dyads." *Journal of Applied Psychology* 65(2):172-175.

Hubbard, F.P. 1979. "Taking persons seriously: A jurisprudential perspective on social disputes in a changing neighborhood." *Cincinnati Law Review* 48(1):15-41.

Hudson, J. and Galaway, B., eds. 1975. *Considering the Victim: Readings in restitution and victim compensation.* Springfield, Ill: C.C. Thomas.

Hudson, J. and Galaway, B. 1977. *Restitution in Criminal Justice: A critical assessment of sanctions.* Lexington, Mass.: Lexington Books/D.C. Heath.

Hudson, J. and Galaway, B., eds. 1978. *Offender Restitution in Theory and Action.* Lexington, Mass.: Lexington Books/D.C. Heath.

Hunsaker, J.S.; Hunsaker, P.L.; and Chase, N. 1981. "Guidelines for productive negotiating relationships." *Personnel Administrator* 26(3):37-40.

Hunt, D.W. 1976. "Medical malpractice arbitration: A comparative analysis." *Virginia Law Review* 62(7):1285-1310.

Hush, H. 1969. "Collective bargaining in voluntary agencies." Social Casework 50(4):210-213.

Hyland, M. 1979. "Comment on Branthwaite, et al.'s mathematical model of intergroup conflict." European Journal of Social Psychology 9(4):417-418.

Hyman, R. 1975. Industrial Relations: A Marxist introduction. London: MacMillan.

Hyman, R. 1978. "Pluralism, procedural consensus, and collective bargaining." British Journal of Industrial Relations 16(1):16-40.

Iannaccone, L. 1979. "The management of decline: Implications for our knowledge in the politics of education." Education and Urban Society 11(3):418-430.

Ichniowski, C. 1982. "Arbitration and police bargaining: Prescriptions for the blue flu." Industrial Relations 21(2):149-166.

Ihinger, M. 1975. "The referee role and norms of equity: A contribution toward a theory of sibling conflict." Journal of Marriage and the Family 37(3):515-524.

Irving, H.H. and Bohm, P.E. 1978. "Social science approach to family dispute resolution." Canadian Journal of Family Law 1(1):39-56.

Jacobson, D. 1981. "Intraparty dissensus and interparty conflict resolution: A laboratory experiment in the context of the Middle East conflict." Journal of Conflict Resolution 25(3):471-494.

Jacobson, N.S. 1978. "Specific and nonspecific factors in the effectiveness of a behavioral approach to the treatment of marital discord." Journal of Consulting and Clinical Psychology 46(3):442-452.

Jamieson, D.W. and Thomas, K.W. 1974. "Power and conflict in the student-teacher relationship." Journal of Applied Behavioral Sciences 10(3):321-326.

Jandt, F.E., ed. 1973. Conflict Resolution through Communication. New York: Harper & Row.

Janis, I.L. and Mann, L. 1977. Decision Making: A psychological analysis of conflict, choice, and commitment. New York: The Free Press.

Jennings, T.W. 1980. "The crossroads of the future." Labor Law Journal 31(8):498-502.

Jensen, J.V. 1978. "A heuristic for the analysis of the nature and extent of a problem." Journal of Creative Behavior 12(3):168-180.

Johnson, E., Jr. 1978. Preliminary Analysis of Alternative Strategies for Processing Civil Disputes. Washington, D.C.: U.S. Department of Justice, LEAA, National Institute of Law Enforcement and Criminal Justice. Los Angeles, Calif.: Program for the Study of Dispute Resolution Policy, University of Southern California Law Center.

Judd, C.M. 1978. "Cognitive effects of attitude conflict resolution." *Journal of Conflict Resolution* 22(3):483-498.

Julian, B.J. 1979. "Effectiveness of a brief treatment program using conflict resolution and contingency management." *Dissertation Abstracts International* 40(1-B):454.

Kagan, S., et al. 1981. "Conflict resolution style among Mexican children examining urbanization and ecology effects." *Journal of Cross-Cultural Psychology* 12(2):222-232.

Kahn, R.L. 1972. "The justification of violence: Social problems and social solutions." *Journal of Social Issues* 28(1):155-175.

Kahn, R.L. and Boulding, E., eds. 1964. *Power and Conflict in Organizations*. New York: Basic Books.

Kahn, R.L.; Wolfe, D.M.; Quinn, R.P.; Snoek, J.D.; and Rosenthal, R.A. 1964. *Organizational Stress: Studies in role conflict and ambiguity*. New York: John Wiley & Sons.

Kaplan, A. 1964. "Power in perspective." In *Power and Conflict in Organizations*, edited by R.L. Kahn and E. Boulding. New York: Basic Books.

Karrass, C.L. 1974. *Give and Take: The complete guide to negotiating strategies and tactics*. New York: Thomas Y. Crowell Co.

Katz, D. 1964. "Approaches to managing conflict." In *Power and Conflict in Organizations*, edited by R.L. Kahn and E. Boulding. New York: Basic Books.

Katz, D. and Kahn, R.L. 1978. *The Social Psychology of Organizations*, 2d ed. New York: John Wiley & Sons.

Kaye, P., et al. *Core Curriculum in Preventing and Reducing School Violence and Vandalism, Course 4: Interpersonal Relations: Participant guide and reference notebook*. Chevy Chase, Md.: Center for Human Services. Washington, D.C.: U.S. Department of Justice, Law Enforcement Assistance Administration, Office of Juvenile Justice and Delinquency Prevention.

Kearns, W.P. 1980. "The development of a marriage enrichment program on conflict management for recently married couples." *Dissertation Abstracts International* 41(3-A):1087.

Keating, J.M., Jr. 1982. "Re-humanizing our institutions: A correctional prescription." *Journal of Intergroup Relations* 10(2):11-23.

Keenan, A. and McBain, G.D. 1979. "Effects of Type A behavior, intolerance of ambiguity, and locus of control on the relationship between role stress and work-related outcomes." *Journal of Occupational Psychology* 52(4):277-285.

Kelley, H.H. 1978. *Personal Relationships: Their structures and processes*. Hillsdale, N.J.: L. Erlbaum Associates.

Kelley, H.H., et al. 1978. "Sex differences in comments made during conflict within close heterosexual pairs." *Sex Roles* 4(4):473-492.

Kennedy, E.M. 1978. "Equal justice and the problem of access." Loyola of Los Angeles Law Review 11(3):485-491.

Kenworthy, A. and Steer, M. 1978. "Social change and the management of conflict: Critical skills for the contemporary program administrator." Education and Training of the Mentally Retarded 13(4):424-426.

Kerr, C. 1954. "Industrial conflict and its mediation." American Journal of Sociology 60(3):230-245.

Kershen, H., ed. 1977. Impasse and Grievance Resolution. Farmingdale, N.Y.: Baywood Publishing Co.

Kessler, S. 1977. Creative Conflict Resolution: Mediation. Atlanta, Ga.: National Institute for Professional Training.

Kettering Foundation. 1979, 1980, 1981. The Negotiated Investment Strategy.

Kidder, R.L. 1975. "Afterword: Change and structure in dispute processing." Law and Society Review 9(2):385-391.

Kilmann, R.H. and Thomas, K.W. 1978. "Four perspectives on conflict management: An attributional framework for organizing descriptive and normative theory." Academy of Management Review 3(1):59-68.

King, D. 1981. "Three cheers for conflict!" Personnel 58(1):13-22.

Klein, D.M. 1979. "Developmental context, coorientation, and conflict management in marriage." Dissertation Abstracts International 39(9-A):5750.

Klier, J. 1979. "Comparison of verbal behaviors and outcome constructiveness between high-adjustment and low-adjustment couples during conflict resolution." Dissertation Abstracts International 39(11-B):5562.

Klimoski, R.J. 1978. "Simulation methodologies in experimental research on negotiations by representatives." Journal of Conflict Resolution 22(1):61-77.

Knudson, R.M.; Sommers, A.A.; and Golding, S.L. 1980. "Interpersonal perception and mode of resolution in marital conflict." Journal of Personality and Social Psychology 38(5):751-763.

Koch, K., ed. 1979. Access to Justice, vol. 4. The Anthropological Perspective/Patterns of Conflict Management: Essays in the ethnography of law. Alphen Aan Den Rijn, Netherlands: Sijthoff and Noordhoff

Kochan, T.A. 1980. "Collective bargaining and organizational behavior research." Research in Organizational Behavior 2:129-176.

Kochan, T.A. and Dyer, L. 1976. "A model of organizational change in the context of union-management relations." Journal of Applied Behavioral Science 12(1):59-78.

Kochan, T.A. and Jick, T. 1978. "The public sector mediation process: A theory and empirical examination." Journal of Conflict Resolution 22(2):209-240.

Kochan, T.A., et al. 1979. *Dispute Resolution under Fact-finding and Arbitration*. New York: American Arbitration Association.

Kolb, D.A.; Rubin, I.; and MacIntyre, J. 1979. *Organizational Psychology: A book of readings*, 3d ed. Englewood Cliffs, N.J.: Prentice-Hall.

※ Kolb, D.M. 1980. "Two approaches to the mediator's role." *Monthly Labor Review* 103(6):38-40.

※ Kolb, D.M. 1981. "Roles mediators play: State and federal practice." *Industrial Relations* 20(1):1-17.

Koron, P.; Carlton, K.; and Shaw, D. 1980. "Marital conflict: Relations among behaviors, outcomes, and distress." *Journal of Consulting and Clinical Psychology* 48(4):460-468.

Korshak, S.R. 1982. "Arbitrating the termination of a union activist." *Personnel Journal* 61(1):54-57.

Kracke, K.R. 1981. "A survey of procedures for assessing family conflict and dysfunction." *Family Therapy* 8(3):241-253.

Kraybill, R.S. 1981. *Repairing the Breach: Ministering in community conflict*. Scottdale, Penn.: Herald Press.

Kressel, K., et al. 1977. "Divorce therapy: An in-depth survey of therapists' views." *Family Process* 16(4):413-443.

Kressel, K., et al. 1977. "Professional intervention in divorce: The views of lawyers, psychotherapists, and clergy." *Journal of Divorce* 2(2):119-155.

※ Kressel, K.; Deutsch, M.; Jaffee, N.; Tuchman, B.; and Watson, C. 1977. "Mediated negotiations in divorce and labor disputes: A comparison." *Conciliation Courts Review* 15(2):9-12.

※ Krislov, J. 1976. "Mediation under the railway labor act: A process in search of a name." *Labor Law Journal* 27(5):310-315.

Krislov, J. and Mead, J. 1981. "Arbitrating union conflicts: An analysis of the AFL-CIO internal disputes plan." *Arbitration Journal* 36(2):21-29.

Kumagai, F. and O'Donoghue, G. 1978. "Conjugal power and conjugal violence in Japan and the USA." *Journal of Comparative Family Studies* 9(2):211-222.

Labovitz, G.H. 1980. "Managing conflict." *Business Horizons* 23(3):30-37.

Lacy, W.B. 1978. "Assumptions of human nature, and initial expectations and behavior as mediators of sex effects in Prisoner's Dilemma research." *Journal of Conflict Resolution* 22(2):269-281.

※ Lake, L.M., ed. 1980. *Environmental Mediation: The search for consensus*. Boulder, Colo.: Westview Press.

Lammers, D.R. 1979. "Relationships between perceptions of self and spouse, marital adjustment, and the negotation of conflict." *Dissertation Abstracts International* 40(3-A):1702.

Landis, B.I. 1977. Value Judgments in Arbitration: A case study of Saul Wallen. Ithaca, N.Y.: New York State School of Industrial and Labor Relations, Cornell University.

Lansbury, R.D. 1978. "Return to arbitration: Recent trends in dispute settlement and wages policy in Australia. International Labour Review 117(5):611-624.

Largay, D.F. 1978. "Self-disclosure and conflict resolution among couples." Dissertation Abstracts International 39(2-A):779.

Lasch, C. 1977. Haven in a Heartless World: The family besieged. New York: Basic Books.

LaTour, S. 1978. "Determinants of participant and observer satisfaction with adversary and inquisitorial modes of adjudication." Journal of Personality and Social Psychology 36(12):1531-1545.

Law Enforcement Assistance Administration. 1974. Citizen Dispute Settlement: An exemplary project. Washington, D.C.: LEAA.

Layne, N.R., Jr., and Balswick, J.O. 1973. Ascension at the Crossroads: A case study of a church caught in the turbulence of rapid social change. Athens: Institute of Community and Area Development, The University of Georgia.

Lebell, D. 1980. "Managing professionals: The quiet conflict." Personnel Journal 59(7):566-572.

Leik, R.K. 1963. "Instrumentality and emotionality in family interaction." Sociometry 26(1):131-145.

Lempert, R. 1978. "More tales of two courts: Exploring changes in the 'dispute settlement function' of trial courts." Law and Society Review 13(1):91-138.

Levens, B.R. and Dutton, D.G. 1980. "Social service role of police: Domestic crisis intervention." Ottawa, Ontario, Canada: United Way of Greater Vancouver, Vancouver, B.C., Canada.

Levi, A.M. and Benjamin, A. 1977. "Focus and flexibility in a model of conflict resolution." Journal of Conflict Resolution 21:406-423.

Levin, E. and De Santis, D.V. 1978. Mediation: An annotated bibliography. Ithaca, N.Y.: New York State School of Industrial and Labor Relations, Cornell University.

Levinger, G. 1957. "Kurt Lewin's approach to conflict and its resolution: A review with some extensions." Journal of Conflict Resolution 1(4):329-339.

Lewis, L.F. 1981. "Conflicting commands versus decision time: A cross-level experiment." Behavioral Science 26(1):79-84.

Li, V.H. 1978. Law without Lawyers: A comparative view of law in China and the United States. Boulder, Colo.: Westview Press.

Liebes, R.A. 1973. "Partisan mediation by the Central Labor Council." Monthly Labor Review 96(9):55-56.

Lightman, E.S. and Irving, H.H. 1976. "Conciliation and arbitration in family disputes." Conciliation Courts Review 14(2):12-21.

Likert, R. and Likert, J.G. 1976. New Ways of Managing Conflict. New York: McGraw-Hill Co.

Likert, R. and Likert, J.G. 1978. "A method for coping with conflict in problem-solving groups." Group and Organization Studies 3(4):427-434.

Lind, E. A.; Erickson, B.E.; Friedland, N.; and Dickenberger, M. 1978. "Reactions to procedural models for adjudicative conflict resolution: A cross-national study." Journal of Conflict Resolution 22(2):318-341.

Lindskold, S. 1978. "Trust development, the GRIT proposal, and the effects of conciliatory acts on conflict and cooperation." Psychological Bulletin 85(4):772-793.

Lippitt, G.L. 1982. "Managing conflict in today's organizations." Training and Development Journal 36(7):66-74.

Lockhart, C. 1979. Bargaining in International Conflicts. New York: Columbia University Press.

Lodato, F.J. 1979. "A view on sports: Vicarious conflict resolution. That's what it's all about." International Journal of Sport Psychology 10(1):52-53.

Lodato, F.J. 1982. "Developing conflict resolution skills." Momentum 13(2):25-27.

Loevi, F.J., Jr. and Kaplan, R.P. 1982. Arbitration and the Federal Sector Advocate: A practical guide, 2d ed. New York: American Arbitration Association.

Loewenberg, J.J.; Gershenfeld, W.J.; Glasbeek, H.J.; Hepple, B.A.; and Walker, K.F. 1976. Compulsory Arbitration: An international comparison. Lexington, Mass.: Lexington Books/D.C. Heath.

London, M. and Howat, G. 1978. "The relationship between employee commitment and conflict resolution behavior." Journal of Vocational Behavior 13(1):1-14.

Long, N.E. 1969. "The local community as an ecology of games." Urban Government: A reader in administration and politics, edited by E.C. Banfield. New York: The Free Press.

Longfellow, C. 1979. "Divorce in context: Its impact on children." Divorce and Separation, edited by G. Levinger and O.C. Moles. New York: Basic Books.

Lowe, J.I. and Herranen, M. 1978. "Conflict in teamwork: Understanding roles and relationships." Social Work in Health Care 3(3):323-330.

Lowy, M.J. 1978. "A good name is worth more than money: Strategies of court use in urban Ghana." In *Disputing Process: Law in ten societies*, edited by L. Nader and H.F. Todd, Jr. New York: Columbia University Press.

Lutzker, D.R. 1961. "Sex role, cooperation and competition in a two-person, non-zero sum game." *Journal of Conflict Resolution* 5(4):366-368.

Madden, M. and Janoff-Bulman, R. 1981. "Blame, control, and marital satisfaction: Wives' attributions for conflict in marriage." *Journal of Marriage and the Family* 43(3):663-674.

Magenau, J.M. and Pruitt, D.G. 1978. "The social psychology of bargaining: A theoretical synthesis." In *Industrial Relations: A social psychological approach*, edited by G.M. Stephenson and C.J. Brotherton. London: Wiley.

*Maggiolo, W.A. 1971. *Techniques of Mediation in Labor Disputes*. Dobbs Ferry, N.Y.: Oceana Publications.

Maines, D.R. 1978. "Structural parameters and negotiated orders: Comment on Benson, and Day and Day." *Sociological Quarterly* 19(3):491-496.

Malouf, M.W.K. and Roth, A.E. 1981. "Disagreement in bargaining: An experimental study." *Journal of Conflict Resolution* 25(2):329-348.

March, J.G. and Simon, H.A. 1958. *Organizations*. New York: John Wiley & Sons.

Marcus, G.E. 1979. "Litigation, interpersonal conflict, and role succession disputes in the friendly islands." In *Access to Justice*, edited by K. Koch. Alphen Aan Den Rijn, Netherlands: Sijthoff and Noordhoff.

Marmo, M. 1980. "Arbitration of mental illness cases." *Labor Law Journal* 31(7):403-416.

Marske, C.E. and Vago, S. 1980. "Law and dispute processing in the academic community." *Judicature* 64(4):165-175.

Mastenbroek, W.F.G. 1980. "Negotiating: A conceptual model." *Group and Organization Studies* 5(3):324-339.

Mayhall, P.D. 1979. *Community Relations and the Administration of Justice*, 2d ed. New York: John Wiley & Sons.

Mazur, A. 1968. "A non-rational approach to theories of conflict and coalitions." *Journal of Conflict Resolution* 12(2):196-205.

M'Bow, A. 1978. "The practice of consensus in international organizations." *International Social Science Journal* 30(4):893-903.

McCarthy, J.E. 1980. "Conflict and mediation in the academy." *New Directions for Higher Education, no. 32 (Resolving Conflict in Higher Education)* 8(4):1-8.

McCarthy, J. and Ladimer, I. 1981. *Resolving Faculty Disputes*. New York: American Arbitration Association.

McCllenahen, J.S. 1975. "Washington's professional peacemakers." <u>Industry Week</u> 184(2):38-42.

McCoy, S. and Glazzard, P. 1978. "Winning the case but losing the child: Interdisciplinary experiences with PL 94-142." <u>Journal of Clinical Child Psychology</u> 7(3):205-208.

McDonald, G.W. 1980. "Family power: The assessment of a decade of theory and research, 1970-1979." <u>Journal of Marriage and the Family</u> 42(4):841-854.

McDonald, W.F. 1976. <u>Criminal Justice and the Victim</u>. Beverly Hills, Calif.: Sage Publications.

McEwen, C.A. and Maiman, R.J. 1982. "Mediation and arbitration: Their problems and performance as alternatives to court." In <u>The Analysis of Judicial Reform</u>, edited by P.L. Dubois. Lexington, Mass: Lexington Books/D.C. Heath.

McGillis, D. 1980. <u>Neighborhood Justice Centers</u>. Cambridge, Mass.: ABT Associates, Inc.; Washington, D.C.: U.S. Department of Justice, National Institute of Justice.

McGillis, D. 1980. "Neighborhood justice centers as mechanisms for dispute resolution." In <u>New Directions of Psycholegal Research</u>, edited by P.D. Lipsett and B.D. Sales. New York: Van Nostrum Reinhold.

McGillis, D. 1980. "The quiet (r)evolution in American dispute settlement." <u>Harvard Law School Bulletin</u> 31(2):20-25.

McGillis, D. and Mullen, J. Oct. 1977. <u>Neighborhood Justice Centers: An analysis of potential models</u>. Washington, D.C.: National Institute of Law Enforcement and Criminal Justice, Office of Development, Testing, and Dissemination.

McGonagle, J.J., Jr. 1972. "Arbitration of consumer disputes." <u>Arbitration Journal</u> 27(2):65-84.

McNeil, E.B., ed. 1965. <u>The Nature of Human Conflict</u>. Englewood Cliffs, N.J.: Prentice-Hall.

McNeil, K. 1978. "Understanding organizational power: Building on the Weberian legacy." <u>Administrative Science Quarterly</u> 23(1):65-90.

Medrano, E. 1979. "An exploratory examination of role conflict, role ambiguity and job related tension experienced by selected non-academic higher education middle managers." <u>Dissertation Abstracts International</u> 39(7-A):4078-4079.

Meeker, R.J. and Shure, G.H. 1969. "Pacifist bargaining tactics: Some 'outsider' influences." <u>Journal of Conflict Resolution</u> 13(4):487-493.

Melton, R.F. 1978. "Resolution of conflicting claims concerning the effect of behavioral objectives on student learning." <u>Review of Educational Research</u> 48(2):291-302.

Merry, S.E. 1979. "Going to court: Strategies of dispute management in an American urban neighborhood." Law and Society Review 13(4):891-925.

Metropolitan Human Relations Commission. 1979. Portland (Oregon): Neighborhood mediation pilot project annual research report, 1979. Portland, Oreg.: MHRC.

Meyers, M.A. 1980. "Social contexts and attributions of criminal responsibility." Social Psychology Quarterly 43(4):405-419.

Miller, S.L. 1973. "Mediation in Michigan." Judicature 56(7):290-294.

Minor, J.H. and Minor, B.J. 1978. "Value conflict resolution: A training model for counselors of minority clients." Journal of Employment Counseling 15(4):164-170.

Mittenthal, R. 1981. "Making arbitration work: Alternatives in designing the machinery." Arbitration Journal 36(3):35-39.

Molnar, J.J. and Rogers, D.L. 1979. "A comparative model of interorganizational conflict." Administrative Science Quarterly 24(3):405-425.

Monchar, P.H. 1981. "Regional educational inequality and political instability." Comparative Education Review 25(1):1-12.

Morley, I.E. and Stephenson, G.M. 1977. The Social Psychology of Bargaining. London: G. Allen & Unwin.

Mueller, R.K. 1978. Career Conflict: Management's inelegant dysfunction. Lexington, Mass.: Lexington Books/D.C. Heath.

Mulvey, E.P. and Reppucci, N.D. 1981. "Police crisis intervention training: An empirical investigation." American Journal of Community Psychology 9(5):527-546.

Murker, W. 1978. "Landlord-tenant disputes and the police." Law Enforcement Quarterly 7(3-4):8-11.

Musser, S.J. 1982. "A model for predicting the choice of conflict management strategies by subordinates in high stakes conflicts." Organizational Behavior and Human Performance 29(1):257-269.

Nader, L. 1979. "Disputing without the force of law." Yale Law Journal 88(4):998-1021.

Nader, L. and Singer, L.R. 1976. "Dispute resolution and law in the future: What are the choices?" California State Bar Journal 51(4):281-286, 311-320.

Nader, L. and Todd, H.F., Jr., eds. 1978. The Disputing Process: Law in ten societies. New York: Columbia University Press.

National School Public Relations Association. 1976. Communicating during Negotiations/Strikes: A communication handbook from the National School Public Relations Association. Arlington, Va.: NSPRA.

Nebgen, M.K. 1979. "Coping with conflict in educational circles." Thrust for Educational Leadership 9(2):25-27.

Neef, M. and Nagel, S. 1974. "The adversary nature of the American legal system from a historic perspective." New York Law Forum 20(1):123-164.

Neil, T.C. 1980. Interpersonal Communications for Criminal Justice Personnel. Boston, Mass.: Allyn and Bacon.

Nejelski, P. 1978. "Court annexed arbitration." Forum 14(2):215-221.

Nejelski, P. 1980. "The 1980 Dispute Resolution Act." Judges' Journal 19(1):33-35, 44-45.

Nelson, N.E. and Curry, E.M. 1981. "Arbitrator characteristics and arbitral decisions." Industrial Relations 20(3):312-317.

Nelson-Horchler, J. 1981. "Keeping consumer cases out of court." Industry Week 208(1):28-30.

Neville, M.K., Jr. 1979. "The enforcement of arbitration clauses in Investor-Broker Agreements." Arbitration Journal 34(1):5-11.

Newman, H.R. 1979. "Mediation and factfinding." In Portrait of a Process: Collective negotiations in public employment, edited by M.K. Gibbons, R.D. Helsby, J. Lefkowitz, and B.Z. Tener. Fort Washington, Pa.: Labor Relations Press.

Nicolau, G. 1978. The Limits and Potential of Environmental Mediation. New York: Institute for Mediation and Conflict Resolution.

Nicolau, G. 1981. "The Institutue for Mediation and Conflict Resolution: A private sector approach to community disputes." Journal of Intergroup Relations 9(2):54-61.

Nicolau, G. and Cormick, G.W. 1972. "Community disputes and the resolution of conflict: Another view." Arbitration Journal 27(2):98-112.

Nierenberg, G.I. 1973. Fundamentals of Negotiating. New York: Hawthorn Books.

Nilsson, T. 1981. "Changes in the work process and labour conflicts in Swedish pharmacies." Acto Sociologica 24(1-2):5-24.

Norland, S.; Shover, N.; Thornton, W.E.; and James, J. 1979. "Intrafamily conflict and delinquency." Pacific Sociological Review 22(2):223-240.

Nye, R.D. 1973. Conflict Among Humans. New York: Springer Publishing Co.

O'Grady, J.P., Jr. 1976. "Grievance mediation activities by state agencies." Arbitration Journal 31(2):125-130.

Ollendick, D.G. 1979. "Loss of control and anxiety as mediating variables of locus of conflict in disadvantaged youth." Journal of Psychology 101(1):23-25.

Olson, D.H. 1969. "The measurement of family power by self-report and behavioral methods." Journal of Marriage and the Family 31(3):545-550.

Olson, D.H. and Rabunsky, C. 1972. "Validity of four measures of family power." Journal of Marriage and the Family 34(2):224-234.

Olson, D.H. and Ryder, R.G. 1970. "Inventory of marital conflicts (IMC): An experimental interaction procedure." Journal of Marriage and the Family 32(3):443-448.

Olson, P.A. 1980. "An investigation of couples' conflict management skills and marital satisfaction." Dissertation Abstracts International 40(12-B):5796.

Oppenheimer, M. 1969. The Urban Guerrilla. Chicago: Quadrangle.

Osmond, M.W. and Martin, P.Y. 1978. "A contingency model of marital organization in low income families." Journal of Marriage and the Family 40(2):315-329.

Palmer, J.W. 1975. "The Night Prosecutor: Columbus finds extrajudicial solutions to interpersonal disputes." Judicature 59(1):22-27.

Palmer, J.W. 1975. "Pre-arrest diversion: The Night Prosecutor's program in Columbus, Ohio." Crime and Delinquency 21(2):100-108.

Pankert, A. 1980. "Settlement of labour disputes in essential services." International Labor Review 119(6):723-737.

Park, C.W. 1978. "A conflict resolution choice model." Journal of Consumer Research 5(2):124-137.

Parnell, P. 1981. "Community justice versus crime control." In Race, Crime, and Criminal Justice, edited by R.R. McNeely and C.C. Pope. Beverly Hills, Calif.: Sage Publications.

Paster, I. 1981. "Collective bargaining: Warnings for the novice negotiator." Personnel Journal 60(3):203-207.

Pauley, R.J. 1975. "Mandatory arbitration of support matters in the family courts." New York State Bar Journal 47(1):27-29, 58-62.

Payne, S.L. 1980. "Organization ethics and antecedents to social control processes." Academy of Management Review 5(3):409-414.

Pelligrino, J.R. 1981. "Teaching stress management: Meeting individual and organizational needs." SAM Advanced Management Journal 46(2):27-30,35-39.

Peterson, D.M. 1969. "Husband-wife communication and family problems." Sociology and Social Research 53(3):375-384.

Pierce, J.T. 1975. "Due process and lay judges." North Carolina Central Law Journal 6(2):339-349.

Pines, B. 1977. "Noncriminal solutions for minor misdemeanor complaints." American Bar Association Journal 63(9):1208-1211.

Pneuman, R.W. and Bruehl, M.E. 1982. *Managing Conflict: A complete process-centered handbook.* Englewood Cliffs, N.J.: Prentice-Hall.

Podemski, R.S. and Steele, R. 1981. "Avoid the pitfalls of citizen committees." *American School Board Journal* 168(4):40-42.

Pompa, G.R. 1981. "The community relations service: Public sector mediation and conciliation of racial disputes." *Journal of Intergroup Relations* 9(2):46-53.

Ponder, L. 1979. "Quality assurance: Managing conflict." *American Corrective Therapy Journal* 33(1):3-8.

Pondy, L.R. 1967. "Organizational conflict: Concepts and models." *Administrative Science Quarterly* 12(2):296-320.

Pondy, L.R.; Fitzgibbons, D.E.; and Wagner, J.A. 1980. *Organizational Power and Conflict: A bibliography.* Monticello, Ill.: Vance Bibliographies.

Pood, E.A. 1978. "Communication and conflict: An experimental study of two types of confrontation behavior in a new conceptual paradigm for the study of conflict." *Dissertation Abstracts International* 38(9-A):5126.

Pood, E.A. 1980. "Functions of communication: An experimental study in group conflict situations." *Small Group Behavior* 11(1):76-86.

Price, T.F. 1978. "Conflict resolution among juvenile delinquents." *Dissertation Abstracts International* 39(5-A):3161.

Pruitt, D. 1971. "Conclusions: Toward an understanding of choice shifts in group discussions." *Journal of Psychology and Social Psychology* 20(3):495-510.

* Pruitt, D.G. 1981. *Negotiation Behavior.* New York: Academic Press.

Pruitt, D.G. and Carnevale, J.D. 1981. "The development of integrative agreements." In *Cooperation and Helping Behavior: Theories and research,* edited by V.J. Derlega and J. Grzelak. New York: Academic Press.

Quevillon, R.P. 1979. "Reactivity of self-monitoring in marital interactions: Effects of goal setting and instructions on verbal behaviors of married dyads." *Dissertation Abstracts International* 40(4-B):1909.

Rahim, A. 1979. "Managing conflict through effective organization design: An experimental study and the MAPS design technology." *Psychological Reports* 44(3):759-764.

Rahim, A. and Bonoma, T.V. 1979. "Managing organizational conflict: A model for diagnosis and intervention." *Psychological Reports* 44(3):1323-1344.

Raiffa, H. 1982. *The Art and Science of Negotiation.* Cambridge, Mass.: The Belknap Press of Harvard University Press.

* Randolph, L.L. 1973. *Third-Party Settlement of Disputes in Theory and Practice.* Dobbs Ferry, N.Y.: Oceana Publications.

Rands, M.; Leringer, G.; and Mellinger, G.D. 1981. "Patterns of conflict resolution and marital satisfaction." Journal of Family Issues 2(3):297-321.

Raven, B.H. 1965. "Social influence and power." In Current Studies in Social Psychology, edited by I.D. Steiner and M. Fishbein. New York: Holt, Rinehart and Winston.

Raven, B.H. and Kruglanski, A.W. 1970. "Conflict and power." In The Structure of Conflict, edited by P. Swingle. New York: Academic Press.

Reichman, M. 1980. "Resolving campus-community conflicts." New Directions for Institutional Advancements (Effective Community Relations) 10(2):79-92.

Reisman, J. 1982. "Technology or politics? Conflict management behavior in public managerial professions." Eugene, Oreg.: Center for Educational Policy and Management, College of Education, University of Oregon.

Renwick, P.A. 1975. "Impact of topic and source of disagreement on conflict management." Organizational Behavior and Human Performance 14(3):416-425.

Renwick, P.A. 1975. "Perception and management of superior-subordinate conflict." Organizational Behavior and Human Performance 13(3):444-456.

Rich, R.C. and Rosenbaum, W.A., eds. 1981. "Citizen participation in public policy." Journal of Applied Behavioral Science 17(4):437-614.

Richert, S.E. 1979. "Waging peace: A global paper on resolving conflict." Social Education 43(4):281-290.

Ridington, J. 1977-78. "The transition process: A feminist environment as reconstitutive milieu." Victimology 2(3-4):563-575.

Rietzes, D.C. and Rietzes, D.C. 1980. "Saul D. Alinsky's contribution to community development." Journal of the Community Development Society 11(2):39-52.

Rifkin, J., et al. 1980. "Legal studies and mediation." In New Directions for Higher Education, no. 32 (Resolving Conflict in Higher Education) 8(4):49-54.

Roark, A.E. and Wilkinson, L. 1979. "Approaches to conflict management." Group and Organization Studies 4(4):440-452.

Robbins, S.P. 1974. Managing Organizational Conflict: A non-traditional approach. Englewood Cliffs, N.J.: Prentice-Hall.

Robbins, S.P. 1978. "'Conflict management' and 'conflict resolution' are not synonymous terms." California Management Review 21(2):67-75.

Robin, A.L. 1981. "A controlled evaluation of problem solving communication training with parent-adolescent conflict." Behavior Therapy 12(5):593-609.

Robins, E. 1972. "Some comparisons of mediation in the public and private sectors." In Collective Bargaining in Government: Readings and cases, edited by J. Joseph Loewenberg and Michael H. Moskow. Englewood Cliffs, N.J.: Prentice-Hall.

Rodgers, R.H. 1973. *Family Interaction and Transaction: The developmental approach*. Englewood Cliffs, N.J.: Prentice-Hall.

Rodriguez, R. 1980. "Final offer arbitration: The role of motivational orientation and intervention strength." *Dissertation Abstracts International* 40(9-B):4572.

Rogers, C.R. 1965. "Dealing with psychological tensions." *Journal of Applied Behavioral Science* 1(1):6-24.

Roll, E.J. 1980. "Psychologists' conflicts about the inevitability of conflict during adolescence: An attempt at reconciliation." *Adolescence* 15(59):661-700.

Rollin, S.A. and Dowd, E.T. 1979. "Conflict resolution: A model for effective marital and family relations." *American Journal of Family Therapy* 7(1):61-67.

Rosenberg, Charles. 1982. "Do it yourself: One way managers solve their own legal problems." *Management* 3:13.

Ross, H.L. and Littlefield, N.O. 1978. "Complaint as a problem-solving mechanism." *Law and Society Review* 12(2):199-216.

Roy, J.O. 1981. "Avoiding conflicts in meetings." *Personnel Journal* 60(9):677.

Rubenstein, L.S. 1976. "Procedural due process and the limits of the adversary system." *Harvard Civil Rights-Civil Liberties Law Review* 11(1):48-96.

Rubin, J.Z. 1980. "Experimental research on third-party intervention in conflict: Toward some generalizations." *Psychological Bulletin* 87(2):379-391.

Rubin, J.Z. and Brown, B.R. 1975. *The Social Psychology of Bargaining and Negotiation*. New York: Academic Press.

Sabalis, R.F. and Ayers, G.W. 1977. "Emotional aspects of divorce and their effects on the legal process." *The Family Coordinator* 26(4):391-394.

Safilos-Rothschild, C. 1976. "The study of family power structure: A review 1960-1969." *Journal of Marriage and the Family* 32(4):539-552.

Salas, L. and Schneider, R. 1979. "Evaluating the Dade County citizen dispute settlement program." *Judicature* 63(4):174-183.

Sarat, A. and Grossman, J.B. 1978. "Courts and conflict resolution: Problems in the mobilization of adjudication." In *American Court Systems, 1978*, edited by Sheldon Goldman and Austin Sarat. San Francisco: W.H. Freeman and Company.

Sayers, S. 1978. *Problem Solving: A five step model--keys to community development series: 3*. Washington, D.C.: National Institute of Education.

Scanzoni, J.H. 1968. "A social system analysis of dissolved and existing marriages." *Journal of Marriage and the Family* 30(3):452-461.

Scanzoni, J.H. 1972. *Sexual Bargaining: Power politics in the American marriage*. Englewood Cliffs, N.J.: Prentice-Hall.

Scanzoni, J.H. and Polonko, K. 1980. "A conceptual approach to explicit marital negotiation." *Journal of Marriage and the Family* 42(1):31-44.

Schafer, R.B. and Keith, P.M. 1980. "Equity and depression among married couples." *Social Psychology Quarterly* 43(4):430-435.

Schafer, S. 1975. "The proper role of a victim-compensation system." *Crime and Delinquency* 21(1):45-49.

Schein, E.H. 1969. *Process Consultation: Its role in organization development*. Reading, Mass.: Addison-Wesley.

Scher, J.M. 1974. "Conflict, negotiation, and cooperation: An analysis of these parameters in national and international relations." *American Journal of Psychotherapy* 28(2):222-234.

Schlenker, B.R. and Bonoma, T.V. 1978. "Fun and games: The validity of games for the study of conflict." *Journal of Conflict Resolution* 22(1):7-38.

Schlenker, B.R. and Goldman, H.J. 1978. "Cooperators and competitors in conflict: A test of the 'triangle model.'" *Journal of Conflict Resolution* 22(3):393-410.

Schmid, H. 1968. "Peace research and politics." *Journal of Peace Research* 5:217-232.

Schmidt, W.H. and Tannenbaum, R. 1960. "The management of differences." *Harvard Law Review* 38(Nov-Dec):107-115.

Schrodt, P.A. 1981. "Conflict as a determinant of territory." *Behavioral Science* 26(1):37-50.

Schroeder, H.W. 1980. "The effect of perceived conflict on evaluations of natural resource management goals." *Dissertation Abstracts International* 41(2-B):676.

Schuetz, J. 1978. "Communicative competence and the bargaining of Watergate." *Western Journal of Speech Communication* 42(2):105-115.

Schwartz, R.D. and Miller, J.C. 1964. "Legal evolution and societal complexity." *American Journal of Sociology* 70(2):159-169.

Scull, A.T. 1977. *Decarceration, Community Treatment and the Deviant: A radical view*. Englewood Cliffs, N.J.: Prentice-Hall.

Sebring, R.H. 1978. "Teacher-administrator conflict: Can it be resolved?" *NASSP Bulletin* 62(415):37-41.

Sebring, R.J. and Duffee, D. 1977. "Who are the real prisoners? A case of win-lose conflict in a state correctional institution." Journal of Applied Behavioral Science 13(1):23-40.

Shapiro, T. 1981. "On the quest for the origins of conflict." Psychoanalytic Quarterly 50(1):1-21.

Shea, G.P. 1980. "The study of bargaining and conflict behavior: Broadening the conceptual arena." Journal of Conflict Resolution 24(4):706-741.

Sheane, D. 1980. "When and how to intervene in conflict." Personnel Journal 59(6):515-518.

Sherif, M. 1958. "Superordinate goals in the reduction of intergroup conflict." American Journal of Sociology 63(4):349-356.

Shockley-Zelabak, P. 1981. "The effects of sex differences on the preference for utilization of conflict styles of managers in a work setting: An exploratory study." Public Personnel Management 10(3):289-295.

Silberman, L.J. 1979. Non-Attorney Justice in the United States: An empirical study. New York: Institute of Judicial Administration.

Simkin, W.E. 1971. Mediation and the Dynamics of Collective Bargaining. Washington, D.C.: Bureau of National Affairs. *[handwritten: list of suggested characteristics of mediators]*

Singer, L.R. 1979. "Growth of nonjudicial resolutions: Speculations on the effects of justice for the poor and on the role of legal services." In Resolution of Minor Disputes. Washington, D.C.: U.S. Congress; House Subcommittee on Courts, Civil Liberties, and the Administration of Justice.

Sinnott, J.D. and Guttmann, D. 1978. "Dialectics of decision making in older adults." Human Development 21(3):190-200.

Skolnick, A.S. 1973. The Intimate Environment: Exploring marriage and the family. Boston: Little, Brown.

Slade, P.D. and Sheekan, M.J. 1979. "The measurement of 'conflict' in repertory grids." British Journal of Psychology 70(4):519-524.

Smith, H.L. 1977. "Threats to the individual." Social Science and Medicine 11(8/9):449-451.

Snyder, F.E. 1978. "Crime and community mediation-The Boston experience: A preliminary report on the Dorchester Urban Court Program." Wisconsin Law Review:737-790.

Spencer, J.M. and Zammit, J.P. 1977. "Reflections on arbitration under the family dispute services." Arbitration Journal 32(2):111-122.

Sprecht, H. 1969. "Disruptive tactics." Social Work 14(2):5-15.

Sprey, J. 1969. "The family as a system in conflict." Journal of Marriage and the Family 31(4):699-706.

Sprey, J. 1971. "On the management of conflict in families." *Journal of Marriage and the Family* 33(4):722-731.

Sprey, J. 1972. "Family power structure: A critical comment." *Journal of Marriage and the Family* 34(2):235-243.

Sprey, J. 1979. "Conflict theory and the study of marriage and the family." In *Contemporary Theories About the Family*, vol. 2, edited by W.R. Burr, R. Hill, F.I. Nye, and I.L. Reiss. New York: The Free Press.

Stamato, L. 1980. "Taking the initiative: Alternatives to government regulation." In *New Directions for Higher Education, no. 32 (Resolving Conflict in Higher Education)* 8(4):55-68.

Stanley, S.F. 1978. "Family education to enhance the moral atmosphere of the family and the moral development of adolescents." *Journal of Counseling Psychology* 25(2):110-118.

Starke, F.A. and Notz, W.A. 1981. "Pre- and post-intervention effects of conventional versus final offer arbitration." *Academy of Management Journal* 24(4):832-850.

Statsky, W.P. 1974. "Community courts: Decentralizing juvenile jurisprudence." *Capital University Law Review* 3(1):1-31.

Stein, D.B. 1978. "Principles of conflict: Revision and reconceptualization." *Dissertation Abstracts International* 39(3-B):1504-1505.

Steiner, H.M. 1978. *Conflict in Urban Transportation: The people against the planners*. Lexington, Mass.: Lexington Books/D.C. Heath.

Steinmann, D.O.; Smith, T.H.; Jurdem, L.G.; and Hammond, K.R. 1977. "Application of social judgment theory in policy formulation: An example." *Journal of Applied Behavioral Science* 13(1):69-88.

Steinmetz, S.K. 1977. *The Cycle of Violence: Assertive, aggressive and abusive family interaction*. New York: Praeger Publishers.

Stephenson, G.M. and Kniveton, B.K. 1978. "Interpersonal and interparty exchange: An experimental study of the effect of seating position on the outcome of negotiations between teams representing parties in dispute." *Human Relations* 31(6):555-566.

Straus, D.B. 1977. *Mediating Environmental, Energy, and Economic Tradeoffs: A case study of the search for improved tools for facilitating the process*. New York: American Arbitration Association.

Straus, D.B. 1978. "Mediating environmental disputes." *Arbitration Journal* 33(4):5-8.

Straus, M.A. 1979. "Measuring intrafamily conflict and violence: The Conflict Tactics (CT) scales." *Journal of Marriage and the Family* 41(1):75-88.

Strauss, A.L. 1978. *Negotiations: Varieties, contexts, processes, and social order*. San Francisco: Jossey-Bass.

Strodtbeck, F.L. 1951. "Husband-wife interaction over revealed differences." *American Sociological Review* 16(4):468-473.

Stulberg, J.B. 1975. "A civil alternative to criminal prosecution." *Albany Law Review* 39(3):359-376.

Stumpf, S.A. 1977. "Using integrators to manage conflict in a research organization." *Journal of Applied Behavioral Science* 13(4):507-517.

Subbarao, A.V. 1978. "The impact of binding interest arbitration on negotiation and process outcome: An experimental study." *Journal of Conflict Resolution* 22(1):79-103.

Sullivan, J.; Peterson, R.B.; Kameda, N.; and Shamada, J. 1981. "The relationship between conflict resolution approaches and trust: A cross cultural study." *Academy of Management Journal* 24(4):803-815.

Sullivan, T. 1980. "The process of industrial arbitration." *Journal of Management Studies* 17(2):185-204.

Sviridoff, M. 1980. "Recent trends in resolving interpersonal, community, and environmental disputes." *Arbitration Journal* 35(3):3-9.

Swierczek, F.W. 1980. "Collaborative intervention and participation in organizational change." *Group and Organization Studies* 5(4):438-452.

Swingle, P.A., ed. 1970. *The Structure of Conflict*. New York: Academic Press.

Swint, J.M. and Nelson, W.B. 1978. "The influence of negotiators' self-interest on the duration of strikes." *Industrial and Labor Relations Review* 32(1):56-66.

Tallman, I. 1970. "The family as a small problem solving group." *Journal of Marriage and the Family* 32(1):94-104.

Temoshok, L.; Riess, B.F.; Rubin, R.; and Leahy, R.L. 1978. "Assessment and training in effective decision making for juveniles in trouble." *Corrective and Social Psychiatry and Journal of Behavior Technology, Methods and Therapy* 24(3):115-132.

Thee, M. 1980. "The China-Indochina conflict: Notes on the background and conflict resolution: The case of neutrality." *Journal of Peace Research* 17(3):223-233.

Thomas, K.W. 1976. "Conflict and conflict management." In *Handbook of Industrial and Organizational Psychology*, edited by M.D. Dunnette. Chicago: Rand McNally.

Thomas, K.W. 1977. "Toward multi-dimensional values in teaching: The example of conflict behaviors." *Academy of Management Review* 2(3):484-490.

Thomas, K.W. 1978. "Introduction: Conflict and the collaborative ethic." *California Management Review* 21(2):56-60.

Thomas, K.W. and Schmidt, W.G. 1976. "A survey of managerial interests with respect to conflict." Academy of Management Journal 19:315-318.

Thomas, K.W. and Pondy, L.R. 1977. "Toward an intent model of conflict management among principal parties." Human Relations 30:1089-1102.

Thomas, K.W.; Jamieson, D.W.; and Moore, R.K. 1978. "Conflict and collaboration: Some concluding observations." California Management Review 21(2):91-95.

Thompson, J.D. 1960. "Organizational management of conflict." Administrative Science Quarterly 4(4):389-409.

Tietze, R.L. 1979. "An investigation of conflict resolution in decision making among married couples with traditional and non-traditional sex-role orientations." Dissertation Abstracts International 39(11-B):5595.

Tighe, C.F. 1980. "Exposure to violence and personality characteristics associated with conflict resolution techniques in intrafamily conflict." Dissertation Abstracts International 40(8-A):4417.

Tjosvold, D. 1978. "Cooperation and conflict between administrators and teachers." Journal of Research and Development in Education 12(1):138-148.

Tjosvold, D. 1980. "Effects of controversy and defensiveness on cognitive perspective-taking." Psychology Reports 47: 1043-1053.

Tjosvold, D. and Deemer, D.K. 1981. "Effects of a control on collaborative orientation on participation in organizational decision making." Canadian Journal of Behavioral Sciences 13(1):33-43.

Toch, H. 1978. "Social climate and prison violence." Federal Probation 42(4):21-25.

Toch, H. 1979. "Alienation as a vehicle of change." Journal of Community Psychology 7(1):3-11.

Torczyner, J. 1978. "Dynamics of strategic relationships." Social Work 23(6):467-474.

Townsend, P.K. 1978. "The politics of mobility among the Sanio-Hiowe." Anthropological Quarterly 51(1):27-35.

Tucker, C.O. and Wilson, G.L. 1980. "Confrontation rhetoric in institutional settings: A rational process." Central States Speech Journal 31(1):42-51.

Turner, R.H. 1970. Family Interaction. New York: John Wiley & Sons.

Twentyman, C.T. and Martin, B. 1978. "Modification of problem interaction in mother-child dyads by modeling and behavioral reversal." Journal of Clinical Society 34(1):138-143.

Twomey, D.F. 1978. "The effects of power properties on conflict resolution." Academy of Management Review 3(1):144-150.

Umana, R.F. 1979. "Clinician predictions of couple abilities to cope with crisis." *Dissertation Abstracts International* 40(4-B):1919-1920.

Updegraff, D.R. 1980. "Role conflict, role ambiguity, and role conflict resolution: A sociological study of middle managers in schools for the deaf." *Dissertation Abstracts International* 40(7-A):4253-4254.

Van de Vliert, E. 1981. "Siding and other reactions to a conflict: A theory of escalation toward outsiders." *Journal of Conflict Resolution* 25(3):495-520.

van Doorn, J.A.A. 1966. "Conflict in formal organizations." In *Conflict in Society*, a Liba Foundation volume, edited by A. de Reuck and J. Knight. London: J.&A. Churchill, Ltd.

Vincent, E. 1980. "Results for conflict: Relative status-field theory, TU actors, 1966-69, an inventory of findings." *Attributes and National Behavior, Part 2: Modern International Relations Monograph Series*.

Vincent, E. 1980. "Results for conflict: Relative status-field theory, TT actors, 1966-69, an inventory of findings." *Attributes and National Behavior, Part 2: Modern International Relations Monograph Series*.

Vincent, E. 1980. "Results for conflict: Relative status-field theory, UU behavior, 1966-69." *Attributes and National Behavior, Part 2: Modern International Relations Monograph Series*.

Vincent, E. 1980. "Results for conflict: Relative status-field theory, UT behavior, 1966-69." *Attributes and National Behavior, Part 2: Modern International Relations Monograph Series*.

Vincent, E. 1980. "Results for conflict: TU behavior, 1966-69." *Attributes and National Behavior, Part 2: Modern International Relations Monograph Series*.

Vincent, J.E. 1980. "Patterns of conflict: Relative status-field theory, UU actors, 1966-69, an inventory of findings." *Attributes and National Behavior, Part 2: Modern International Relation Monograph Series*. Gainesville: University of Florida Press.

Vincent, E. and Tindell, J.O. 1969. "Alternative cooperative strategies in a bargaining game." *Journal of Conflict Resolution* 13(4):494-510.

Wall, J.A., Jr. 1981. "Mediation: An analysis, review, and proposed research." *Journal of Conflict Resolution* 25(1):157-180.

Wallace, M. 1979. "Conflict regulation in the industrial sphere: An indirect test of Dahrendorf's theory." *Sociological Focus* 12(3):229-238.

Walton, R.E. 1965. "Two strategies of social change and their dilemmas." *The Journal of Applied Behavioral Science* 1(2):167-179.

Walton, R.E. 1968. "Interpersonal confrontation and basic third-party functions: A case study." *Journal of Applied Behavioral Science* 4(3):327-344.

Walton, R.E. 1969. *Interpersonal Peacemaking: Confrontations and third-party consultation*. Reading, Mass.: Addison-Wesley.

Walton, R.E. 1973. "How to choose between strategies of conflict and collaboration." In *Sensitivity Training and the Laboratory Approach*, edited by R.T. Golembiewski and A. Blumberg. Itasca, Ill.: Peacock.

Walton, R.E. and Dutton, J.M. 1969. "The management of interdepartmental conflict: A model and review." *Administrative Science Quarterly* 14(1):73-84.

Walton, R.E. and McKersie, R. 1965. *A Behavioral Theory of Labor Negotiations*. New York: McGraw-Hill Co.

Walton, R.E. and Warwick, D.P. 1973. "The ethics of organization development." *Journal of Applied Behavioral Science* 9(6):681-698.

Warehime, R.G. 1980. "Conflict-management training: A cognitive/behavioral approach." *Group and Organization Studies* 5(4):467-476.

Warner, C.T. and Olson, T.D. 1981. "Another view of family conflict and family wholeness." *Family Relations* 30(4):493-503.

Warschaw, T.A. 1980. *Winning by Negotiation*. New York: McGraw-Hill Co.

Watkins, T.R. 1979. "Staff conflicts over use of authority in residential settings." *Child Welfare* 58(3):205-215.

Weber, G.H. and McCall, G.J., eds. 1978. *Social Scientists as Advocates: Views from the applied disciplines*. Beverly Hills, Calif.: Sage Publications.

Wedge, B. 1971. "A psychiatric model of intercession in intergroup conflict." *Journal of Applied Behavioral Science* 7(6):733-761.

Weekes, B. 1979. "A.C.A.S.: An alternative to law?" *Industrial Law Journal* 8(3):147-159.

Weeks, J.A. 1979. "The relationship between conflict management behaviors of principals and organizational climate as perceived by principals and teachers in selected Texas public school districts." *Dissertation Abstracts International* 39(7-A):3973-3974.

Wehr, P. 1979. "Environmental peacemaking: Problem, theory, and method." *Research in Social Movements, Conflicts, and Change* (2):63-82.

Wehr, P. and Washburn, M. 1976. *Peace and World Order Systems: Teaching and Research*. Beverly Hills, Calif.: Sage Publications.

Weider-Hatfield, D. 1981. "A unit in conflict management communication skills." *Communication Education* 30(3):265-273.

Wexler, R. 1973. "Court-ordered consumer arbitration." *Arbitration Journal* 28(3):175-184.

Wickstom, R.A. 1979. "Participation revisited: Who decides, when, and how much." *Canadian Administrator* 19(2):1-4.

Wilkening, E.A. 1968. "Toward further refinement of the resource theory of family power." Sociological Focus 2(2):1-19.

Williams, K.R. and Drake, S. 1980. "Social structure, crime, and criminalization: An empirical examination of the conflict perspective." The Sociological Quarterly 21(4):563-575.

Willis, J. 1979. "Sentencing alternatives involving community service-First report of the Sentencing Alternatives Committee." Law Institute Journal 53(10):570-574.

Wilson, K.G. 1978. "A test of the interactionist theory of conflict management." Dissertation Abstracts International 39(3-A):1253.

Witty, C.J. 1980. Mediation and Society: Conflict management in Lebanon. New York: Academic Press.

Wolf, P. 1978. "International social structure and the resolution of international conflicts, 1920-1965." Research in Social Movements, Conflicts and Change (1):35-59.

Wolkinson, B.W. and Liberson, D.H. 1982. "The arbitration of sex discrimination grievances." The Arbitration Journal 37(2):35-44.

Yelen, D.R. 1979. "The resolution of approach-avoidance conflict." Journal of Research in Personality 13(3):326-350.

Yelsma, P. 1981. "Conflict predispositions: Differences between happy and clinical couples." The American Journal of Family Therapy 9(2):57-63.

Young, O., ed. 1975. Bargaining: Formal theories of negotiation. Urbana: University of Illinois Press.

Zambito, S.A. 1980. "Confronting frustration within a school system." NASSP Bulletin 64(439):74-84.

Zammuto, R.F.; London, M.; and Rowland, K.M. 1979. "Effects of sex on commitment and conflict resolution." Journal of Applied Psychology 64(1):91-95.

Zartman, I.W., comp. 1976. The 50% Solution: How to bargain successfully with hijackers, strikers, bosses, oil magnates, Arabs, Russians, and other worthy opponents in this modern world. Garden City, N.Y.: Anchor Press.

Zartman, I.W. 1982. The Practical Negotiator. New Haven, Conn.: Yale University Press.

Zimmerman, A.R. 1978. "The effects and effectiveness of a communication-oriented workshop in marital conflict resolution." Dissertation Abstracts International 39(6-A):3228-3229.

Zirkel, P.A. and Lutz, J.G. 1981. "Characteristics and functions of mediators: A pilot study." Arbitration Journal 36(2):15-20.

Zwingle, J.L. 1980. "Resolving conflict in the upper echelons." <u>New Directions for Higher Education</u>, no. 32 (<u>Resolving Conflict in Higher Education</u>) 8(4):33-42.